iGlobal™

Educational Services
Believe. Inspire. Transform.

GED

Math Study Guide

iGlobal GED Math Study Guide

To order, contact
iGlobal Educational Services, LLC
PO Box 94224
Phoenix, AZ 85070

Website: www.iglobaleducation.com

Fax: 512-233-5389

HOW TO USE THIS STUDY GUIDE

iGlobal Educational Services created this study guide to help you review mathematical concepts that may help you increase your knowledge of topics that may be covered on the GED Exam.

This study guide should be used to supplement strong and viable curriculum that encourages differentiation for all diverse learners. They can be used at home, in tutoring sessions, or at school.

TABLE OF CONTENTS

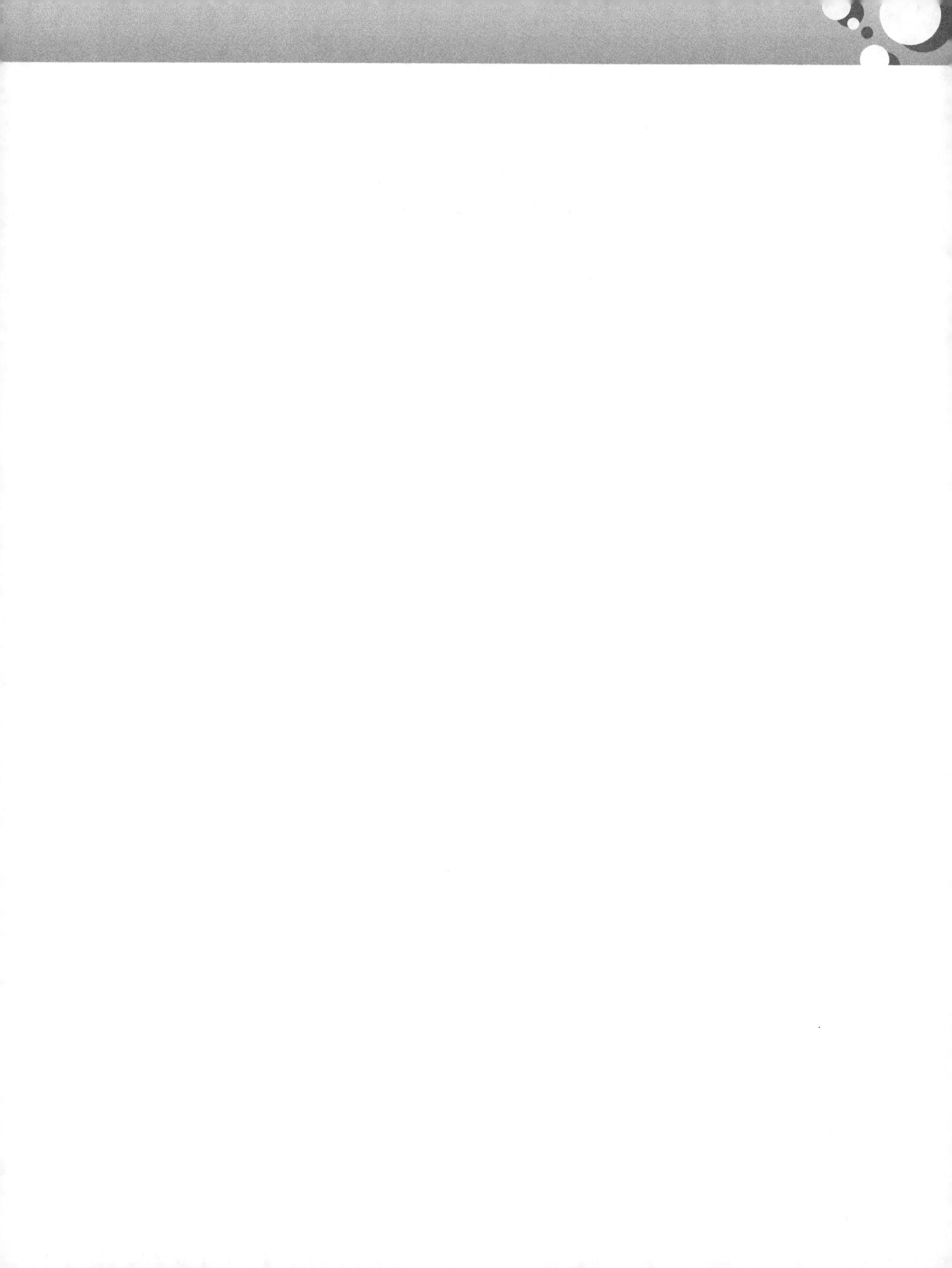

EQUATIONS OF A LINE AND THE GEOMETRY OF TRIANGLES AND RECTANGLES

What You Need to Know

We are going to look at the equations of a line and it application in rates and proportions. By defining a line, we will be able to look at the slope of a line which is the requirement is describing the equations of a straight line. The slope will also enable us classify some straight lines. We will proceed to look at the features of a straight line and also a few curves. Finally, we will look at some few properties of a triangle and a rectangle in relation to their area and perimeter.

MATH TOPICS

- Use the Pythagorean Theorem to determine unknown side lengths in a right triangle. (Reference 1.1).
- Determine the slope of a line from a graph, equation, or table (Reference 1.2).
- Interpret unit rate as the slope in a proportional relationship (Reference 1.3).
- Graph two-variable linear equations (Reference 1.4).
- For a function that models a linear or nonlinear relationship between two quantities, interpret key features of graphs and tables in terms of quantities, and sketch graphs showing key features given a verbal description of the relationship. Key features include: intercepts, intervals where the function is increasing, decreasing, positive, or negative, relative maximums and minimums, symmetries, end behavior, and periodicity (Reference 1.5).
- Write the equation of a line with a given slope through a given point (Reference 1.6).
- Use slope to identify parallel and perpendicular lines and to solve geometric problems (Reference 1.7).
- Locate points in the coordinate plane (Reference 1.8).
- Solve multistep, arithmetic, real-world problems using ratios or proportions including those that require converting units of measure (Reference 1.9).
- Compute the area and perimeter of triangles and rectangles. Determine side lengths of triangles and rectangles when given area or perimeter (Reference 1.10).

INTRODUCTION

The world is a place of interactions and interrelations. Get one item or a variable them you will be shown another one which influences it existence and behavior patterns. For instance, it is obvious that for a soccer team to win, the players must have had quality training, motivation, good last days' preparation and so on. Thus, the variable winning is affected by the quality of training, degree of motivation among other things. If we consider only two variables; the winning and the quality of motivation (consisting of motivation from the team managers and the funs) then we can have data for such a team in various matches come up with a graph and also a model, an equation relating the two variables. To do all these, we need to understand the concept of coordinates and features of straight and curved lines. A closer concepts to these problem may be to investigate and come up a suitable size of a football pitch or distances between opposite vertices of these so that one can come up with a standard measurements. These are the preliminary activities when designing such a facility. In this section, we are going to equip you with the mathematical tools that can enable you carry out all these activities.

USING THE PYTHAGOREAN THEOREM

Any line segment is space or on a plane can be associated with three or two other lines are perpendicular to one another. Having this concept in mind makes it possible to determine the size of such lines. We will consider only lines in a plane. A good example of this situation is a right triangle whose longest side, the hypotenuse, is associated with a base and a height. The length of these three sides are related based on a formula called Pythagorean Theorem.

The theorem for a case of a right triangle states that if c is the hypotenuse, b the base and a the height, then

$$c^2 = b^2 + a^2$$

EXAMPLE 1 ....

The longest side of a right triangle is 15 in. If one of the shorter sides triangle 6 in less than the hypotenuse, find the length of the third side.

EXPLANATION

Hypotenuse (longest side), $c = 15$ in

One of the shortest side, $b = 15 - 6 = 9$ in

The other side, $a = ?$

Using Pythagorean Theorem, we have

$$15^2 = 9^2 + a^2$$
$$225 = 81 + a^2$$
$$a^2 = 225 - 81 = 144$$
$$a = \sqrt{144} = 12 \text{ in}$$

The other side measures 12 in

(we only take the positive value because length is a positive measure)

EXAMPLE 2..

A sales man would like to access some items on the wall 4 feet above the floor of the ware house. If he has to a use a 5 feet ladder, how far should the ladder be from the foot the wall?

EXPLANATION

We assume that the floor is perpendicular to the wall so that the ladder, the distance from the ladder to the wall on the floor and the vertical distance from the foot of the wall to the ladder form a right triangle with the ladder being the hypotenuse.

Thus hypotenuse = 5 feet

Height, a, = 4 feet

Base, b, = ?

$$5^2 = 4^2 + a^2$$
$$25 = 16 + a^2$$
$$a^2 = 25 - 16 = 9$$
$$a = \sqrt{9} = 3 \text{ feet}$$

The ladder should be 3 feet from the wall

SLOPE OF A LINE

The slope of a line is a measure of how steep a line is. A higher slope implies the line is very steep while a smaller slope implies that a line has a gentle slope. When a line is horizontal, its slope is usually zero. On the same note, the slope of a vertical line does not exists, that is, it cannot be defined.

The slope is given by

$$\text{slope} = \frac{\text{rise}}{\text{run}} = \frac{\text{Change in vertical distance}}{\text{change in horizontal distance}} = \frac{\Delta y}{\Delta x}$$

Data is usually represented inform of a table, a graph or summarized using an equation. Since these are the most typical cases, we learn how to determine the slope of a line from these three cases.

Slope from a table

Given a table representing a linear relation, we can identify any two pair of points and use them to find the slope.

EXPLANATION

Find the slope of a linear relation given in the table below if y represents the dependent variable and x the independent variable.

x	0	2	6	16	20
y	−1	4	14	39	49

We pick any two pairs of numbers in the form (x, y).

We can take the second pair and the last pair, that is (2, 4) and (20, 49)

$$\text{Slope} = \frac{\text{rise}}{\text{run}} = \frac{\Delta y}{\Delta x} = \frac{49-4}{20-2} = \frac{45}{18} = \frac{5}{2} = 2.5$$

Thus, the slope is 2.5

Slope from an equation

Equations of straight lines can be transformed to a form $y = mx + c$ where m and c are constants. In that form, the value of m, the coefficient of x, is the slope of a line.

EXAMPLE 2...

Find the slope of a line whose equation is given by $6x - 3y = 20$

EXPLANATION

The equation is transformed as follows

$$6x - 3y = 20$$
$$6x - 20 = 3y$$
$$y = \frac{6}{3}x - \frac{20}{3} = 2x - \frac{20}{3}$$

Hence $y = 2x - \frac{20}{3}$. Comparing with $y = mx + c$, we get that the slope, $m = 2$.

Slope from a graph

When given a graph, we identify the coordinates of two points on the line then use them to determine the slope.

EXAMPLE 3...

Find the slope of the line in the graph below

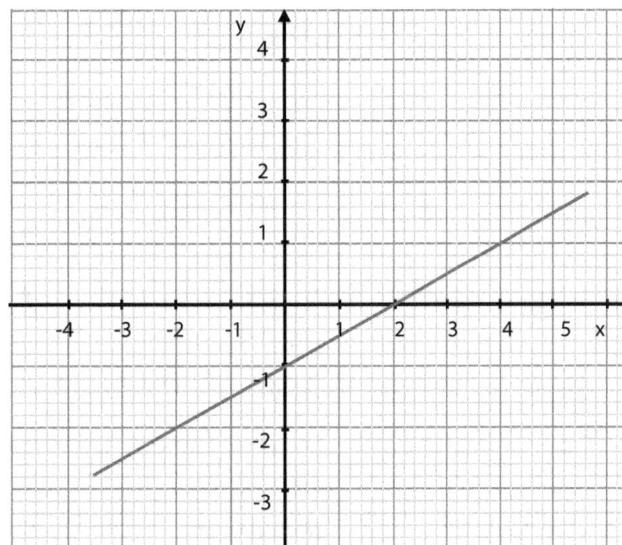

EXPLANATION

We identify the two points of the graph

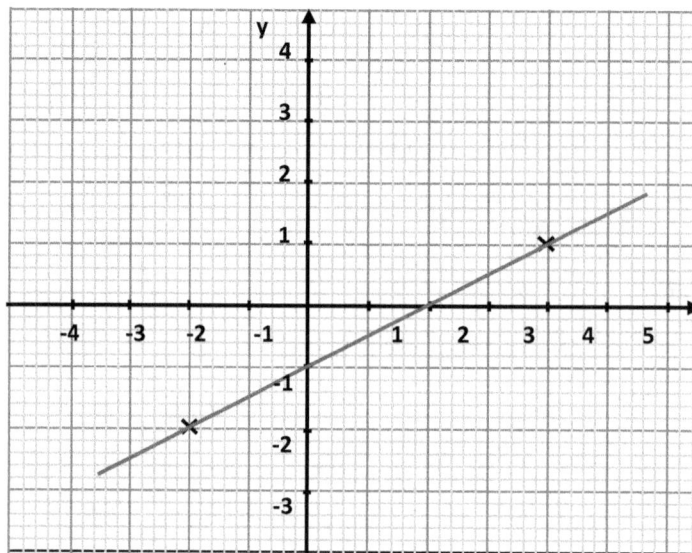

For our case, we have identified (−2, −2) and (4, 1). The slope will

$$\text{Slope} = \frac{\text{rise}}{\text{run}} = \frac{\Delta y}{\Delta x} = \frac{1--2}{4--2} = \frac{3}{6} = \frac{1}{2} = 0.5$$

The slope is 0.5

UNIT RATES AS SLOPE

Rate is a quotient of two variables that are not similar but related. For instance, distance and time covered by a moving object. Unit rates which imply change is a variable 1 per unit variable 2 is a typical case of a slope of a graph.

$$\text{Slope} = \frac{\text{change in } y \text{ values}}{\text{change in } x \text{ values}}$$

A situation where change in x values is a unit (1), then change in y values is the slope which implies a unit rate.

For instance, if we say a car travels at a speed of 50miles per hour, then we are taking about a unit rate where the distance 50miles is covered in one hour. This can be graphically interpreted as a slope of a graph of distance against line. The main property of this graph is that it passes through the origin. The relation leads to yet another concept, proportionality. We say that distance is **directly proportional** to time taken and the constant of proportionality is 50miles/hour, the speed. If d is the distance and t time, we write

$$d = mt$$

where $m = 50$ mi/hr.

EXAMPLE 1 ....

The table below shows the distance covered by a vehicle in different times. Determine the unit rate of the motion.

Distance(mi)	0	46	92	138	184
Time(hr)	0	1	2	3	4

EXPLANATION

Since within the first hour it covers a distance of 46mi, the unit rate = 46mi/hr

EXAMPLE 2 ....

The graph below shows the amount of cash got from the sales of novels, of the same title, to different people. Determine the unit price of the novel.

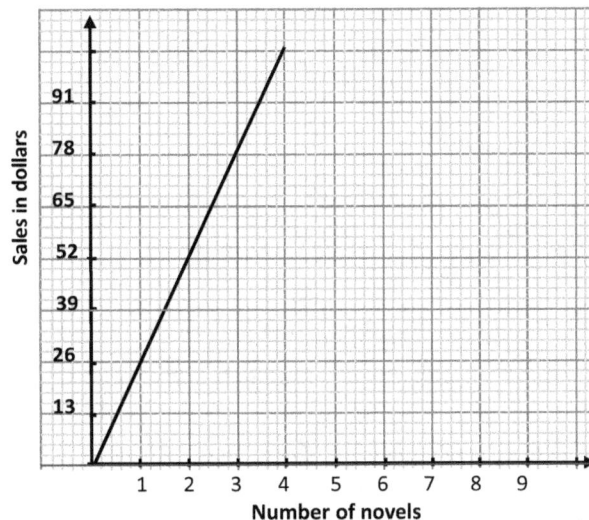

EXPLANATION

Since the graph passes through the origin, the unit sales is the sales (y value) when the number of novels is 1. The number is 26.

Thus, the price is $26 per novel

TWO-VARIABLE LINEAR EQUATIONS

Linear equations generally have two variables, the independent variable, x, and the dependent variable, y. It is only in special cases where such graphs have one variable only. We discuss the procedure of graphing a two variable linear equation.

Given a linear equation in two variables, we identify suitable values of x (independent variable) then use them to get the corresponding y values (dependent variables). From the list, we form a list of at least 2 pairs of x and y values then use them to plot the graph.

EXAMPLE 1 ....

Draw the graph of $3x - 4y - 12 = 0$

EXPLANATION

We make y the subject of the formula first.

$$4y = -3x - 12$$

Dividing through by 4, we get

$$y = -\frac{3}{4}x - \frac{12}{4} = -\frac{3}{4}x - 3$$

When

$$x = 0, y = 0 - 3 = -3$$

When

$$x = -4,$$

$$y = \left(-\frac{3}{4}x - 4\right) - 3 = 3 - 3 = 0$$

The ordered pairs are (0, −3) and (−4,0)

We then plot the points and connect them to have the following graph.

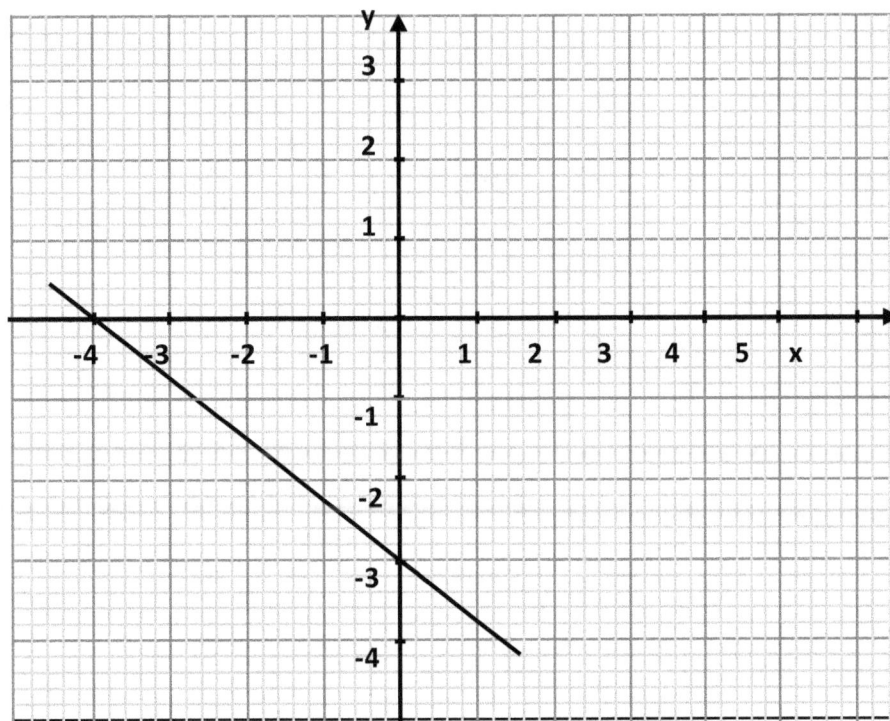

FUNCTIONS

Functions are relations where no two or more values in the output set are associated with one element in the input set. There are many types of functions, linear and other that are broadly classified as nonlinear. These functions have some features that identifies them; these features are the intercepts, slope, and intervals when the function is increasing, decreasing, positive, or negative, relative maximums and minimums, symmetries, end behavior, and periodicity.

Linear functions

These are equations of the form $Ax + By + C = 0$. To study their features, their equations are put in the slope intercept form $y = mx + c$ where m is the slope and c the y intercept. It can also be written in the form

$$\frac{x}{a} + \frac{y}{b} = 1$$

Where a and b are the x and y intercepts respectively.

EXAMPLE 1 ....

Find the y intercept, x intercept and slope of the equation $2y - 3x = 12$.

EXPLANATION

If we divide through by 12, we have

$$\frac{2y}{12} - \frac{3x}{12} = 1$$

$$\frac{y}{6} - \frac{x}{4} = 1$$

Or

$$\frac{y}{6} + \frac{x}{-4} = 1$$

The y intercept is $y = 6$ and the x intercept is $x = -4$.

In slope intercept form, we have $2y = 3x + 12$ or

$$y = \frac{3}{2}x + 6$$

Thus, the slope is $\frac{3}{2}$.

Quadratic functions

These are equations of the form $ax^2 + bx + c = 0$. their features includes the x intercepts which are called the roots, the y intercept, vertex and the line of symmetry since they are symmetrical. They also have the maximum or the minimum points. In the equation above, if $a \geq 0$, then the equation has a minimum point and if $a < 0$, the equation has a maximum point. To find the line of symmetry, we put the equation into the vertex form, that is $y = a(x - p)^2 + q$ where (p, q) is the vertex and $x = p$ is the line of symmetry. The maximum value is therefore $y = q$. The end behavior of this graph can be described. $a < 0$, the end points of the graph points downwards while if $a \geq 0$, the end points (of the graph) points upwards.

EXAMPLE 2..

Find all features of the function $y = 2x^2 + 4x - 7$

EXPLANATION

Intercepts.

At the y intercept, $x = 0$ hence we have $y = -7$.

The y intercept is -7

x intercepts (roots)

At x intercept, $y = 0$. Thus we have $2x^2 + 4x - 7 = 0$.

Using the quadratic formula, we have

$$x = \frac{-4 \pm \sqrt{4^2 - 4 \times 2 \times -7}}{4} = \frac{-4 \pm \sqrt{16 + 42}}{4} = \frac{-4 \pm \sqrt{58}}{4}$$

$$= \frac{-4 \pm 7.616}{4}$$

Thus, we have

$$x = \frac{-4 - 7.616}{4} = -2.904$$

and

$$x = \frac{-4 + 7.616}{4} = 0.904$$

The roots (the x intercepts) are $x = -2.904$ and $x = 0.904$.

The vertex (minimum) and the symmetric line

We put the equation $y = 2x^2 + 4x - 7$ in the vertex form. We have

$$y = 2(x^2 + 2x) - 7$$

We the complete the square in the bracket

$$y = 2(x^2 + 2x + 1) - 7 - 2$$

Using quadratic identity $a^2 + 2ax + b^2 = (a + b)^2$, we have

$$y = 2(x + 1)^2 - 7 - 2$$

We finally have

$$y = 2(x+1)^2 - 9$$

Thus,

The vertex is (−1, −9)

The line of symmetry is $x = -1$

Since $a = 2 > 0$, the function has a minima and appear at point (−1, −9) hence the minimum value of the function is $y = -9$.

The end points

Since $a = 2 > 0$, the graph has a minima hence the end points of the graph points upwards.

Trigonometric functions

These are functions expressed in terms of trigonometric functions. They have different key features. One of them is periodicity which implies the recurrence/oscillation nature of the graphs. The period P of a sine or cosine function is given by $\frac{2\pi}{b}$ where b is the horizontal compression or stretch factor.

That is $y = d\, \sin(bt) + c$ or $y = d\, \cos(bt) + c$.

EXAMPLE 3..

Find the period of $y = \cos t$ and $y = 2\sin\dfrac{t}{2} + 3.$

EXPLANATION

$$y = \cos t = \cos bt$$

Thus, $b = 1$

$$\text{Period is } \frac{2\pi}{1} = 2\pi$$

$$y = 2\sin\frac{t}{2} + 3 = 2\sin bt + 3$$

Thus, $b = \dfrac{1}{2}$

$$\text{Period is } 2\pi \div \frac{1}{2} = 2\pi \times 2 = 4\pi.$$

EQUATION OF A LINE

The equation of a line is an algebraic expression describing a collection of points falling on the line. The most common approach on determining the equation of a line is the use of the definition of a slope. We will approach this by an example.

EXAMPLE 1 ....

Find the equation of a line passing through (−2, 3) whose slope is −2.

EXPLANATION

Slope of the line is −2.

If we take a general point (x, y) and (−2, 3) to be on the line, then slope is

$$\text{slope} = \frac{y-3}{x+2} = -2$$
$$y - 3 = -2(x + 2)$$
$$y - 3 = -2x - 4$$
$$y = -2x - 4 + 3$$
$$y = -2x - 1$$

The equation $y = -2x - 1$

EXAMPLES 2 ....

Find the equation a line passing through (2, 6) and (−4, 5).

EXPLANATION

We first determine the slope

$$\text{slope} = \frac{5-6}{-4-2} = -\frac{1}{6}$$

If we take a general point (x, y) and any of the points given, say (2, 6).

$$\text{slope} = \frac{y-6}{x-2} = -\frac{1}{6}$$

Cross multiplying, we get

$$6y - 36 = -x + 2$$
$$6y = -x + 2 + 36$$
$$6y = -x + 38$$

SLOPE AND PARALLEL AND PERPENDICULAR LINES

The slope of lines tells us a lot about the nature of lines; that is if they are slant, vertical or horizontal. Furthermore, they also tell us if the lines are parallel, perpendicular or otherwise.

For Instance, when two or more lines are parallel, then their slope will be equal and when two lines are perpendicular, then the product of their slopes will be −1.

EXAMPLE 1 ....

Find the slope of the line perpendicular to the line whose equation is given by $7y + 21x - 3 = 0$.

EXPLANATIONS

We change the form of the equation to $y = mx + c$

$7y + 21x - 2 = 0$ becomes $7y = -21x + 3$

Divining through by 7, we get

$$y = -3x + \frac{3}{7}$$

Comparing with $y = mx + c$, we get that the slope is $m = -3$.

If m_2 is the slope of the other line then $m_2x - 3 = -1$, hence , $m_3 = 3$.

The slope of the line is 3.

EXAMPLE 2...

Identify all lines in the list that are parallel to $2y = 3 - 2x$.

$$y = -x + 8$$
$$y - x = 1$$
$$5(y - x) = 20$$
$$7y + 3 = 7x$$
$$3x + 3y = 6$$

EXPLANATION

We determine the slope of each line by converting the equation to the form slope - intercept form.

First, we determine the slope of the given line

$2y = 3 - 2x$ implies $y = \dfrac{3}{2} - x$ hence the slope of the line is –1.

We therefore identify lines whose slope is –1.

$$y = -x + 8$$
$$y = -x + 8 = -1x + 8$$

hence $m = -1$.

The slope is –1 thus equal to the slope of the line given hence parallel

$$y - x = 1$$

$y - x = 1$ implies $y = x + 1 = 1x + 1$. The slope is 1 which is not equal to that of the given line, –1. Thus, not parallel.

$$5(y - x) = 20$$

$5(y - x) = 20$, dividing through by 5, we get $y - x = 4$ which reduces to $y = x + 4$. The slope is 1 which is not equal to that of the given line, -1. Thus, not parallel.

$$7y + 3 = 7x$$

$7y + 3 = 7x$ becomes $7y = 7x - 3$ which becomes $y = x - \dfrac{3}{7}$. The slope is 1 which is not equal to that of the given line, –1. Thus, not parallel.

$$3x + 3y = 6$$

$3x + 3y = 6$ becomes $3y = -3x + 6$ or $y = -x + 2$. The slope is –1 which is equal to that of the given line, –1. Thus, parallel.

Therefore, the lines parallel to $2y = 3 - 2x$ are $y = -x + 8$ and $3x + 3y = 6$.

LOCATING POINTS IN THE COORDINATE PLANE

The location of points on *xy* plane is governed by the concept of coordinates. Coordinates on an *xy* plane refers to the shortest distance from the axes of the *xy* plane. We have *x* and *y* coordinates. The *x*–coordinate the is shortest distance from the vertical axis (*y* axis) while the *y*-coordinate is the shortest distance from the *x* axis. The coordinates of a point are given as a pair in the form (*x, y*) where *x* is the *x* coordinate and *y* is the *y* coordinates.

EXAMPLE 1 ....

Locate the following points on the xy plane. *A*(–3, –1) *B*(2, 4)

EXPLANATION

A(–3, –1) implies 3 units on the left hand side of the *y* axis and 1 unit below the *x* axis. The point is shown below.

B(2, 4) implies 3 units on the right hand side of the *y* axis and 4 unit above the *x* axis. The point is shown below.

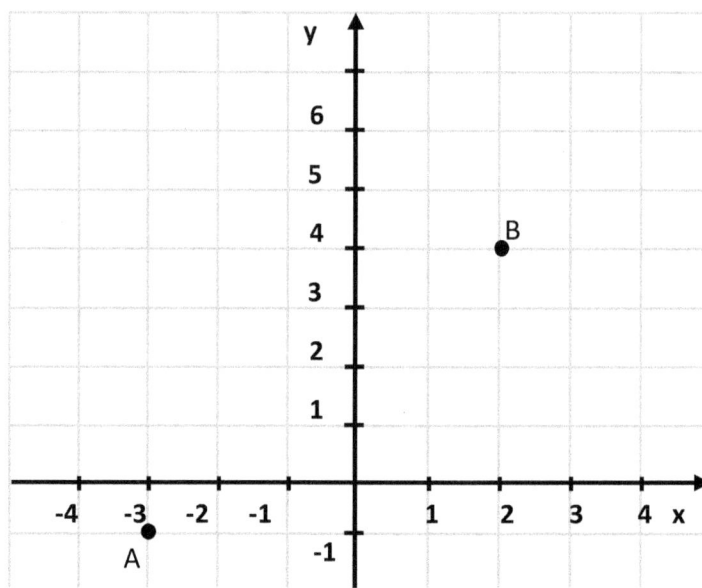

EXAMPLE 2...

Find the coordinates of the points *P. Q* and *R*.

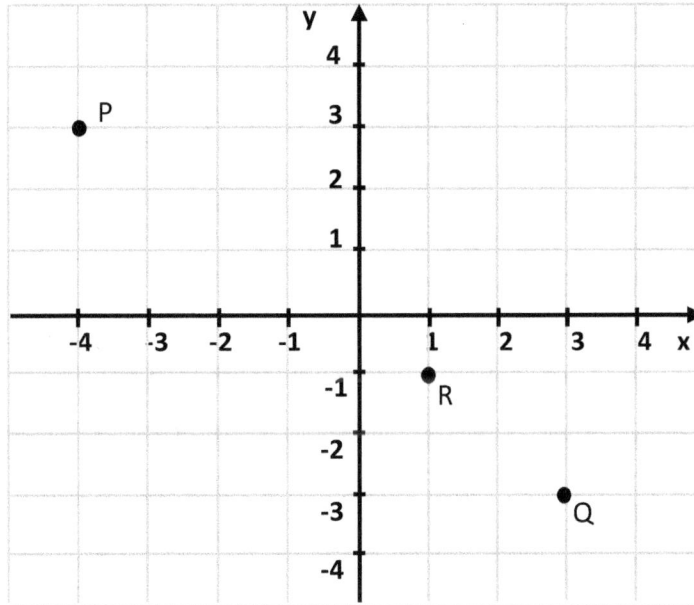

EXPLANATION

Point *P* is 4 units to the left of *y* axis and 3 units above the *x* axis hence the coordinates of P is $P(-4, 3)$.

Point *R* is 1 units to the right of the *y* axis and 1 units below the *x* axis hence the coordinates of *R* is $(1, -1)$.

Point *Q* is 3 units to the right of *y* axis and 3 units below the *x* axis hence the coordinates of *Q* is $Q(3, -3)$.

PROBLEM SOLVING WITH RATIOS AND PROPORTIONS

A ratio is a quotient that of two items that are similar. Since the items are similar, it does not have units. The ratio of two items *c* and *d* is given as $c : d$ or $\frac{c}{d}$ or *c* to *d*. When two ratios are equated, we call the set up a proportion. There are two types of proportions. These are direct and indirect or inverse proportion. To variables x and y are directly proportional if $x \propto y$ which implies $x = py$ where *p* is the constant of proportionality. Two variables *x* and *y* are inversely proportional if $x \propto \frac{1}{y}$ which implies that $x = \frac{q}{y}$ or $xy = q$ where *q* is the constant of proportionality.

EXAMPLE 1 ....

Linus and Stalin contributed a total of $320,000 to start a business. If Stallin contributed 80,000 more than Linus, find the ratio of Stalin to Linus contribution.

EXPLANATIONS

Let Linus' contribution by x

Stalin's contribution is $x + 80,000$

The sum is the total contribution.

Thus
$$x + x + 80000 = 32000$$
$$2x = 240000;[$$
$$x = 120000$$

Stalin's contribution $= x + 80,000 = 120000 + 80000 = 200000$

The ratio of Stalin to Linus contribution is $200000 : 80000 = 5 : 2$.

EXAMPLE 2 ....

The price of three gallons of gasoline $9.9. How much will a person pay to get 7 gallons of gasoline?

EXPLANATION

Since for every increase in the number of gallons bought, the amount increases, the two have a direct proportion given by $p = kx$ where p is the price, x is number of gallons and k the constant of proportionality.

When $p = \$9.9$, $x = 3$ hence we have $9.9 = 3k$.

$$k = \frac{9.9}{3} = 3.3$$

Thus $p = 3.3x$.

When $x = 7$, we have $p = 3.3 \times 7 = \$23.1$.

EXAMPLE 3...

It takes 12 days for 4 people working at the same rate to build a perimeter wall. How longer will such two people take?

Explanation

When the number of people working increases, the time taken decreases hence the two are inversely related. Let

$$p = \frac{k}{t}$$

Where p is the number of people, t the time taken and k the constant of proportionality?

When $p = 4$, $t = 12$ hence

$$4 = \frac{k}{12}$$

And $k = 4 \times 12 = 48$.

Thus

$$p = \frac{48}{t}.$$

If $p = 2$, then $2 = \frac{48}{t}$ or $t = \frac{48}{2} = 24$ hours.

It takes $24 - 12 = 12$ more hours.

AREA AND PERIMETER OF TRIANGLES AND RECTANGLES

A triangle is a polygon having three sides. There are four most common triangles that is Isosceles, scalene, right triangle and equilateral triangle. Isosceles triangle has two sides equal, Equilateral triangle has all sides equal, scalene has none of the sides equal and right triangle two sides meeting perpendicularly. The perimeter of a triangle is the sum of the length of all the three sides.

Area of a triangle is $\frac{1}{2}ab$ where a and b are base and heights respectively, of the triangle.

A rectangle is a quadrilateral having opposite sides equal and parallel. All the sides of a rectangle are perpendicular. Is *l* and *w* are the length (longest side) and w the width (shortest length) then then

Perimeter = $2(l + w)$

Area = lw

EXAMPLE 1 ....

Find the area of a rectangle if its perimeter and width are 28 in and 9 inches respectively.

EXPLANATION

Let *l* and *w* be the length and the width respectively.

$$2(l + w) = 2(9 + w) = 28$$
$$18 + 2w = 28$$
$$2w = 28 - 18 = 10$$
$$w = \frac{10}{2} = 5 \text{ in}$$

Area = $lw = 9 \times 5 = 45$ sq.in

Find the area of a triangular piece of land in form of right triangle if the longest side of the piece of land is 25 yards and one of the shortest side is 7 yards.

Since the piece of land is in form of a right triangle, we use the Pythagorean theorem

Let c, b and d be the sides with c being the hypotenuse, then

$$c^2 = b^2 + d^2$$

Thus,

$$25^2 = 7^2 + d^2$$
$$d^2 = 625 - 49$$
$$d^2 = 576$$
$$d = \sqrt{576} = 24 \text{ yards}$$

We take the positive value only.

$$\text{Area} = \frac{1}{2}ab = \frac{1}{2} \times 24 \times 7 = 84 \text{ sq. yards}$$

WRAPPING IT UP

In this section, we have looked at coordinates of points and slopes of lines which led to the equations of lines. We have seen how slopes can be used to describe some special lines such as parallel and perpendicular lines. About equations of lines, we saw how we can determine it and also relate the equation of a line with the unit rate and how this is related to ratio and proportion. We have also looked at various features of function among them, the intercepts, slope, end behavior, maximum and minimum point among other features. Finally, we have also looked at rectangles and triangles by discussing their perimeter and area and how we can apply Pythagorean Theorem on them.

PERIMETER, AREA AND VOLUME

What You Need to Know About This Section?

In this section, we will discuss the area and the perimeter of plane figures, which are circle and the polygons. Polygons refers to plane figures with three or more sides such as triangles, quadrilaterals and pentagon among others. We will then proceed to discuss the volume and surface area of three dimensional objects such are prisms, pyramids and the sphere. We will finally discuss the concepts of rate, ratio and proportion.

MATH TOPICS

- Compute the area and circumferences of circles. Determine the radius or diameter when given area or circumference (Reference 1.11).
- Compute the perimeter of a polygon. Given a geometric formula, compute the area of a polygon. Determine side lengths of the figure when given the perimeter or area. (Reference 1.12).
- Compute perimeter and area of 2-D composite geometric figures, which could include circles, given geometric formulas as needed. (Reference 1.13).
- When given geometric formulas, compute volume and surface area of rectangular prisms. Solve for side lengths or height, when given volume or surface area. (Reference 1.14).
- When given geometric formulas, compute volume and surface area of cylinders. Solve for height, radius, or diameter when given volume or surface area. (Reference 1.15).
- When given geometric formulas, compute volume and surface area of right prisms. Solve for side lengths or height, when given volume or surface area. (Reference 1.16).
- When given geometric formulas, compute volume and surface area of right pyramids and cones. Solve for side lengths, height, radius, or diameter when given volume or surface area. (Reference 1.17).
- When given geometric formulas, compute volume and surface area of spheres. Solve for radius or diameter when given the surface area. (Reference 1.18).

✍ Compute surface area and volume of composite 3-D geometric figures, given geometric formulas as needed. (Reference 1.19).

✍ Solve one-step or multi-step arithmetic, real world problems involving the four operations with rational numbers, including those involving scientific notation. (Reference 1.20).

INTRODUCTION

In day to day life, we meet quadrilaterals like rectangles, circles and three dimensional figures such as rectangular prisms, pyramids, sphere and others in so many ways. For instance, most cakes are made inform of cylinders or rectangular prisms, the football in made inform of a sphere, the front shape of most windows and doors of houses are inform of a rectangle or a composite figure consisting a rectangle and a semicircle. The latter is common in churches and hotels. There is, therefore, need to understand the perimeter, area and volumes of these figures so that we can create items in form of these figures. Therefore, in this section, we are going to discuss how we can determine the perimeter, area and volumes of these figures. We will further look at ratios, proportions and rates which is also related to the concepts covered in the first sections.

AREA AND CIRCUMFERENCE OF CIRCLES

The circumference of a circle refers to the distance covered around it. It is given by the formula $C = 2\pi r = \pi D$ where D is the diameter, r the radius of the circle and π a constant which is approximated by 3.142, in most cases. Note that twice radius is equal to the diameter.

Sometimes, we may have a fraction of the circle. This may be a half, a quarter or generally a sector of a circle. A sector is a figure that is enclosed by a two radii and an arc of the circle. The angle where the two radii intersects at the center of the circle (called the central angle) is very important since it tells us what fraction of the circle the sector is.

Below are the diagrams of a half circle (also called semicircle), quarter circle and a general sector.

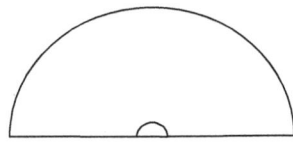

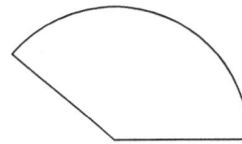

Semicircle	Quarter circle	A sector of circle
(A special sector)	(A special sector)	(A sector whose central angle is an obtuse angle)

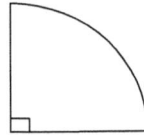

The circumference or perimeter of a sector is given by $\frac{\theta}{360} \times 2\pi r + 2r$ where θ is the central angle of the sector. When using the diameter, then perimeter of a sector is given by

$$\frac{\theta}{360} \times \pi D + D$$

EXAMPLE 1 ....

Find the circumference of circle of radius 7.5 in.

EXPLANATION

The circumference is given by $C = 2\pi r$

We have $r = 7.5$ in and $\pi = 3.142$

Upon substitution, we get $C = 2\pi r = 2 \times 3.142 \times 7.5 = 47.13$ in

EXAMPLE 2..

Find the perimeter of a sector of radius 12 in and central angle 60°.

EXPLANATION

Radius = 12 in hence diameter, D = 12 × 2 = 24 in

Central angle θ = 60°

Perimeter of a sector is given by

$$\frac{\theta}{360} \times \pi D + D = \frac{60}{360} \times 3.142 \times 24 + 24$$
$$= 12.57 + 24$$
$$= 36.72 \text{ in}$$

Area of a circle

The area of a circle is given by πr^2 where r is the radius. For the case of a sector, the area is given by $\frac{\theta}{360} \times \pi r^2$ where θ is the central angle of the sector.

EXAMPLE 3...

Harris has a circular flower garden whose diameter is 2 yards. How big is his flower garden?

EXPLANATION

We find the area of his flower garden.

$$\text{Diameter} = 2.2 \text{ yards hence radius, } r = 1.1 \text{ yard}$$

$$\text{Area} = \pi r^2 = \pi \times 1.1^2 = 3.802 \text{ sq. yards}$$

EXAMPLE 4...

A minute-hand of a clock wipes through an area of 28.29 sq. inches. Determine the length of the minute-hand.

EXPLANATION

Since the minute-hand goes round, it wipes through an area that is enclosed by the circle whose radius is the length of the minute-hand.

Let the radius be r

$$\text{Area} = \pi r^2 = 28.29$$

$$r^2 = \frac{28.29}{\pi} = \frac{28.29}{3.142} = 9.004$$

To get r, we take the square root on both sides $r = \sqrt{9.004} = 3.001 \approx 3.000$

Thus the length of the minute-hand is 3 inches

GEOMETRIC FORMULAS: AREA OF POLYGONS

A polygon is a geometric figure with three sides and above. The most common polygons are triangles, quadrilaterals (4 sided figures), pentagon (5 sided figures), hexagon (6 sided figures) and a above.

Triangles

Area of a triangle whose base is *b* and height is *h*, then the area is

$$Area = \frac{1}{2}bh$$

Quadrilaterals

This refers to four sided figures. They are square, rectangle, rhombus, trapezoid, parallelogram and a kite.

The area of a square of side *s* is given by s^2.

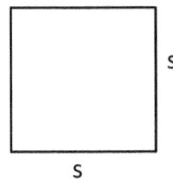

Square

The area of a rectangle of length and width *l* and *w* respectively is given by *lw*

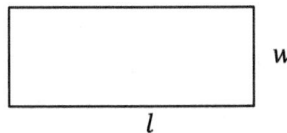

Rectangle

The area of a rhombus or a parallelogram of height *h* and base *b* is given by *bh*

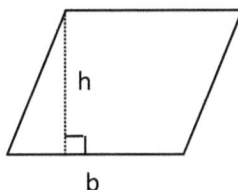

Rhombus

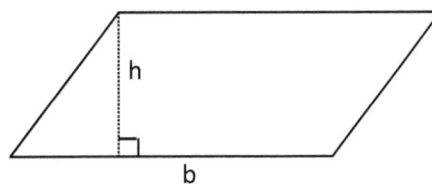

Parallelogram

The area of a trapezoid whose parallel sides area a and b respectively and hight h is given by

$$\frac{1}{2}h(a+b)$$

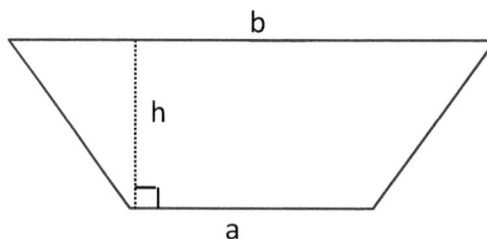

Trapezoid

The area of a kite whose diagonals are given by

$$\frac{1}{2}ab$$

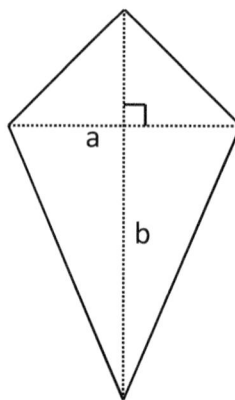

Kite

We proceed by stating a formula for determining the area of polygons that are regular. By regular polygon, we mean a polygon whose sides are all equal. Denote a by the shortest length from the center of the polygon to its side. This length is perpendicular to any side of the polygon and is called the apothem.

The area of regular polygon is therefore given by

$$\frac{1}{2}ap$$

Where a and p are the apothem and the perimeter of the polygon.

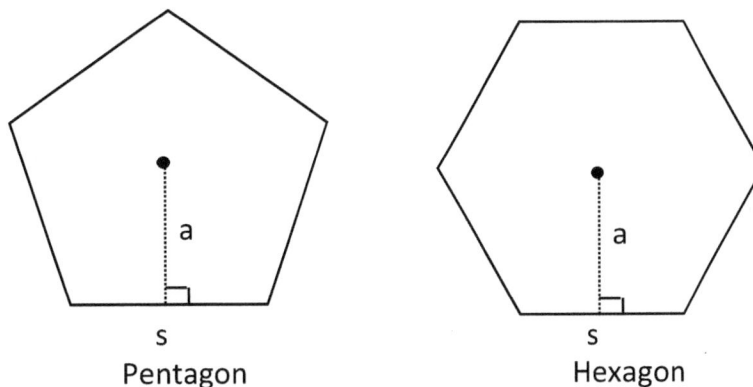

Pentagon   Hexagon

Perimeter $p = sn$ where n is the number of sides of the polygon

EXAMPLE 1 ....

The area of a rectangle is 48 in. If its length is 8 in, determine its width.

EXPLANATION

Let the width be w

Since the length is 8 in

$$\text{Area} = lw = 48$$

Upon substitution, we have

$$8w = 48; \quad w = \frac{48}{8} = 6 \text{ in}$$

EXAMPLE 2 ....

The area of a right triangle is 60 sq. in. If the base is 15 in, find the perimeter of the triangle.

EXPLANATION

The area of a triangle of base b and height a is given by $\frac{1}{2}ab$

From the question, we have area = 60sq. in and $b = 15$ in

Upon substitution, we have

$$\frac{1}{2} \times 15a = 60; \quad 15a = 120$$

Thus

$$a = \frac{120}{15} = 8 \text{ in}$$

Since it is a right triangle, the base and the height are perpendicular hence hypotenuse is determined using the Pythagorean Theorem, hypotenuse $= \sqrt{a^2 + b^2}$

$$\text{Hypotenuse} = \sqrt{8^2 + 15^2} = \sqrt{289} = 17 \text{ in}$$

Perimeter is the sum of the measurement of the sides $= 17 + 8 + 15 = 40$ in

EXAMPLE 3...

Find the area of a kite like piece of farm whose opposite vertices are 10 yards and 18 yards apart.

EXPLANATION

The diagonals of the kite like piece of farm are $a = 10$ yards and $b = 18$ yards respectively

$$\text{The area} = \frac{1}{2}ab = \frac{1}{2} \times 10 \times 18 = 90 \text{ sq. yards}$$

PERIMETER AND AREA OF 2-D COMPOSITE GEOMETRIC FIGURES

Composite geometric figures are plane figures that are composed of more than one basic geometric figure. For instance, we may have a triangle fused together with a rectangle and so on.

To determine the area of a composite figure, we add up the area of the individual basic figures in it.

The perimeter is determined by adding the length of its sides.

EXAMPLE 1 ....

Find the perimeter of the following figure below.

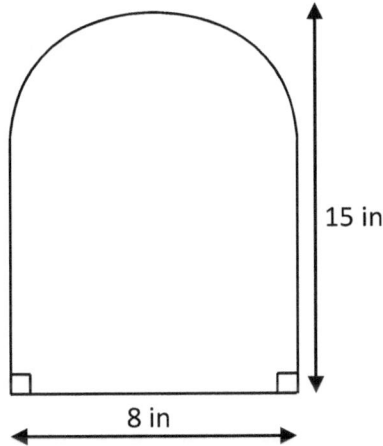

15 in

8 in

EXPLANATION

The figure is composed of a rectangle and a semicircle of diameter 8 in. Therefore, its radius is 4 inches. By including the dotted lines as shown, we can find the length of the rectangle.

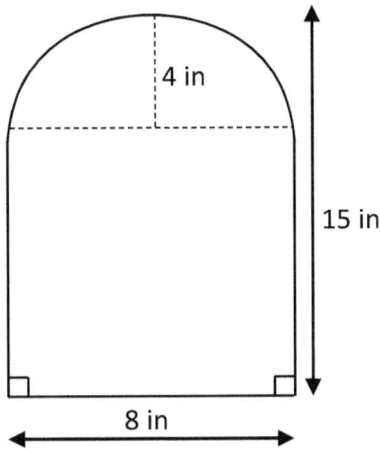

4 in

15 in

8 in

Thus, the length of the rectangle is 14 − 4 = 11 in

The perimeter is the sum of sides of the figure, thus we add the length twice, the width once and the length of an arc which is a semicircle.

Thus length of the arc, C is

$$\frac{\pi D}{2} = \frac{3.142 \times 8}{2} = 12.57 \text{ in}$$

$$\text{The perimeter} = 12.57 + 11 + 8 + 11 = 42.57 \text{ in}$$

EXAMPLE 2...

Find the area of the following figure

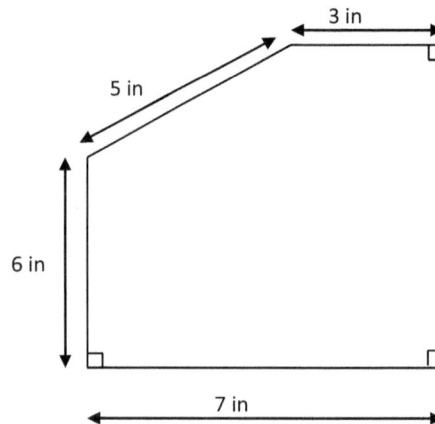

EXPLANATION

We divide the figure into basic geometric shapes, which is trapezoid and the rectangle.

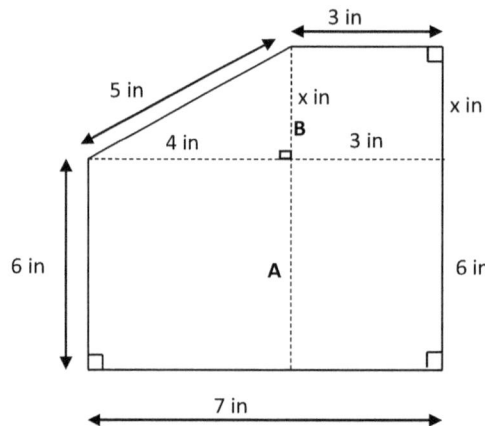

Dividing the figure and assigning the measurements using the properties of rectangles.

To determine, x, we use the Pythagorean Theorem.

$$x = \sqrt{5^2 - 3^2} = \sqrt{16} = 4 \text{ in}$$

Thus, the length of rectangle A is 7 in and the width is 6 in while the parallel sides of the trapezoid B are 7 in and 3 in respectively while its height is 4 in.

We now proceed to determine the area.

$$\text{Area} = \text{area of A} + \text{area of B} = (7 \times 6) + \frac{1}{2} \times 4(3 + 7) = 13 + 20 = 33 \text{ sq. units}$$

EXAMPLE 3..

Find the area of the figure below.

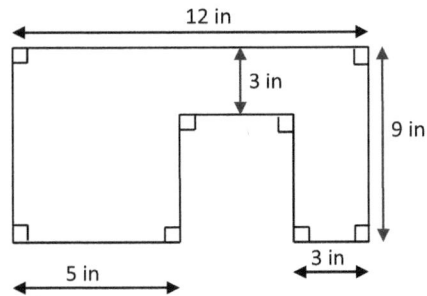

EXPLANATION

We divide the figure into basic geometric figures as shown below

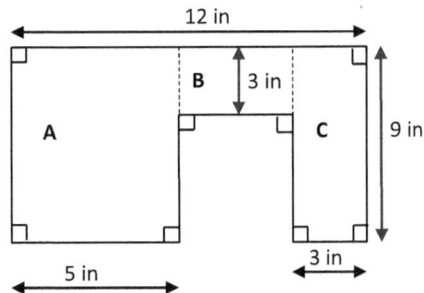

The area of the figure is the sum of the area of A, B and C.

Since horizontal lengths must add up to the same figure, the length of rectangle B is

$$12 - 5 - 3 = 4 \text{ in}$$

Thus are = area of A + area of B + area of C

$$= (5 \times 9) + (4 \times 3) + (3 \times 4)$$
$$= 45 + 12 + 12$$
$$= 69 \text{ sq. in}$$

GEOMETRIC FORMULAS: VOLUME AND SURFACE AREA OF RECTANGULAR PRISMS

A rectangular prism is three dimensional figure with six faces that are all rectangles. The basic dimensions that make up a prism are the length, *l*, the width, *w*, and the height, *h*.

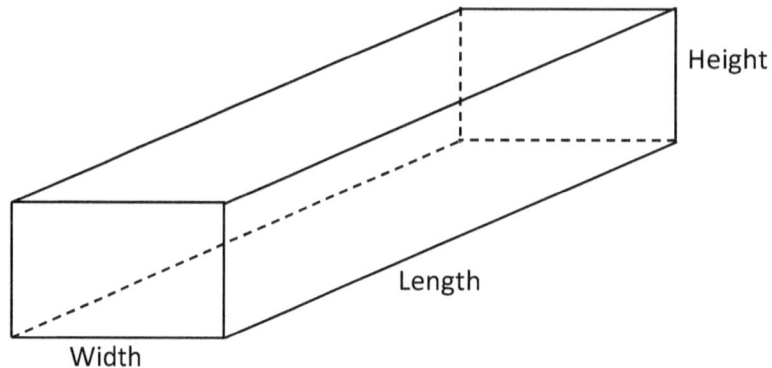

The volume of the rectangular prism is given by *lwh*

Since each face appear twice, that is the top and the bottom faces are the equal, the front and the rear faces are equal and side faces are equal, we have the surface area = 2*lw* + 2*wh* + 2*lh*

EXAMPLE 1 ....

Find the surface area of a rectangular prism of length 12in, width 10 in and height 9 in.

EXPLANATION

We have *l* = 12 in, *w* = 10 in, *h* = 9 in

$$\text{The surface area} = 2lw + 2wh + 2lh = 2(12 \times 10) + 2(12 \times 9) + 2(10 \times 9)$$
$$= 240 + 216 + 18$$
$$= 636 \text{ in}^2$$

EXAMPLE 2 ....

A water tank is in form of a rectangular prism of internal length, width and height of 7 feet, 6 feet and 4 feet respectively. If the tank is a third full, find the capacity of the tank that is empty.

EXPLANATION

We have $l = 7$ feet, $w = 6$ feet, $h = 4$ feet

Volume of the tank is $lwh = 7 \times 6 \times 4 = 168$ cubic feet

The volume of water in the tank us

$$\frac{1}{3} \times 168 = 56 \text{ cubic feet}$$

The volume of the tank that is empty $= 168 - 56112$ cubic feet

EXAMPLE 3..

A mason wishes to plaster the interior of an open rectangular prism tank of 6 feet length by 5 feet width by 4 feet height. If costs \$23 to plaster one square feet, find the cost of plastering the interior of the tank.

EXPLANATION

Since the tank is open, there are only five faces to plaster, that is the side faces and the bottom face.

$$l = 6 \text{ feet}, w = 5 \text{ feet}, h = 4 \text{ feet}$$

The total surface area will be given by

$$\text{Area} = lw + 2wh + 2lh = (6 \times 5) + 2(5 \times 4) + 2(6 \times 4)$$
$$= 30 + 40 + 48$$
$$= 118 \text{ sq. feet}$$

GEOMETRIC FORMULAS: VOLUME AND SURFACE AREA OF CYLINDERS

A cylinder is a three dimensional figure with a curved surface that is enclosed by two circular faces at the top and the bottom. Let r be the radius of the top and the bottom surfaces and h be the height of the cylinder, then the volume is given by $\pi r^2 h$.

Since it is enclosed by three faces, the surface area is the sum of the area of the two faces. The top and the bottom faces are equal with a radius of say r hence, their area will be $2\pi r^2$

The curved surface is inform of a rectangle when cut along it height. Thus, the width of the rectangle is h and the length of the rectangle will be circumference of the top or bottom faces which is $2\pi r$ thus its area is $2\pi rh$.

Therefore, the surface area of a cylinder is given by $2\pi r^2 + 2\pi rh = 2\pi r(r + h)$

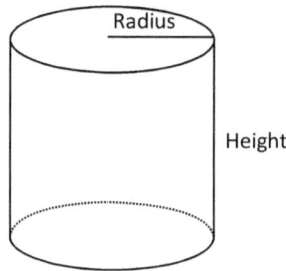

EXAMPLE 1 ....

The volume of a cylinder is 50.5 in³. Find the radius of the bottom face of the cylinder if its height is 4 in.

EXPLANATION

$$\text{Volume} = \pi r^2 h = 50.5$$

If the height = 4, we use the formula above to find the volume

$$\pi r^2 h = 50.5; \quad r^2 = \frac{50.5}{\pi h}$$

$$r^2 = \frac{50.5}{3.142 \times 4} = 4.018 \text{ in}$$

$$r^2 = 4.018; \quad r = 2.005 \text{ in}$$

EXAMPLE 2...

Find the surface area of a closed cylinder of diameter 12 in and height 9 in.

EXPLANATION

A closed cylinder has two circular faces at the top and bottom and a curved surface.

The area of the curved surface is $2\pi rh$

That of the area of circles is $2\pi r^2$

Since diameter = 12 in implying radius is 6 in; height = 9 in

iGlobal GED Math Study Guide

We have

$$2\pi r^2 + 2\pi rh = 2\pi r(r+h)$$
$$= 2 \times 3.142 \times 6(6+9)$$
$$= 2 \times 3.142 \times 90$$
$$= 565.6 \text{ in}^2$$

GEOMETRIC FORMULAS: VOLUME AND SURFACE AREA OF RIGHT PRISMS

A prism is a three dimensional object with a uniform base section (or cross section) along its length. The uniform cross section can be a rectangle, a triangle or any other polygon. It is called a right prim if all the faces along its length are perpendicular to the base face.

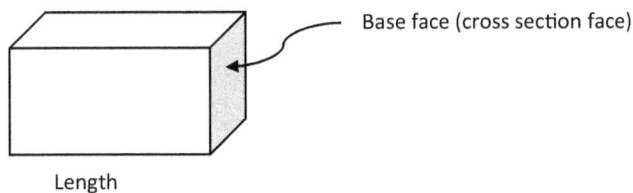

Rectangular based prism

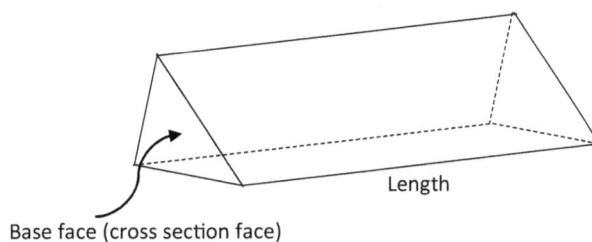

Triangular based prism

The volume of the right prism is given by $BA \times L$

Where BA is the base area and L the length.

The surface area of the right prism is the sum of the area of its faces.

EXAMPLE 1 ....

Find the surface area of a triangular prism of length 14 in and base in form of an equilateral triangle of side 8 in.

EXPLANATION

A triangular based prism has two equilateral triangles, and three rectangles which are the faces along its length.

The length of the rectangles are 14 in each and their width is 8 in since the width are the sides of the equilateral triangle.

Thus, the total area of faces along the length is $3 \times (14 \times 8) = 336$ sq. in

From the equilateral triangle, we divide it into two equal parts to have two 30-60-90 right angle triangle whose hypotenuse, height and base are in the ratio $2 : \sqrt{3} : 1$.

Since 1 is equivalent to half the side, we have the base 30-60-90 right angle triangle $= \frac{1}{2} \times 8 = 4$ in.

Height is equivalent to $\sqrt{3}$ which is $4\sqrt{3} = 5.196$ in

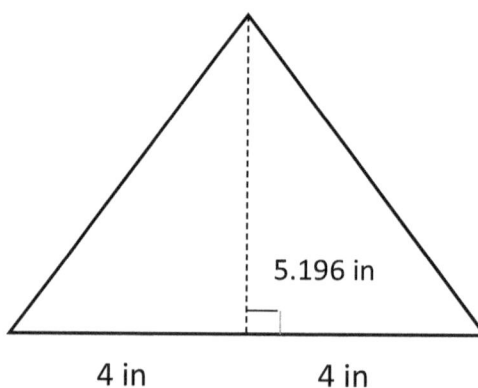

4 in   4 in

Area of the two triangles =

$$\frac{1}{2}bh \times 2 = \frac{1}{2} \times 8 \times 5.196 \times 2 = 41.57 \text{ sq. in}$$

Total surface area $= 41.57 + 336 = 377.57$ sq. in

EXAMPLE 2...

The volume of a square based prism is 735 sq. in. If the length of the prism is 15 in, find the length of one side of the base.

EXPLANATION

$$\text{Volume} = B.A \times L = 735$$

$$L = 15 \text{ in}$$

Thus

$$B.A = \frac{735}{15} = 49$$

The base area is a square whose area $= s^2 = 49$ where is the side of the square.

Thus $s = \sqrt{49} = 7$ in

One side of the base measures 7 in

- When given geometric formulas, compute volume and surface area of right pyramids and cones. Solve for side lengths, height, radius, or diameter when given volume or surface area. (Reference 1.17).

GEOMETRIC FORMULAS: VOLUME AND SURFACE AREA OF RIGHT PYRAMIDS AND CONES

A prism is a three dimensional object with a base and the common apex where all the vertical faces join together. If the perpendicular line from the apex (the height) passes through the center of the base, the prism is referred to as a right pyramid. Based on the base of the pyramid we get the names of the pyramid; thus, square based pyramid, triangular based pyramid (also called a tetrahedron), square based pyramid, rectangular based pyramid among others. A cone is a special pyramid whose base is a circle.

The volume of a pyramid is given by $\frac{1}{3}BA \times H$ where BA is the base area and H the perpendicular height.

The surface area = area of the base + area of the vertical faces.

For a right pyramid, all the vertical faces are equal.

$$\text{Volume of a cone} = BA \times H = \frac{1}{3}\pi r^2 h$$

Surface area of a cone $= \pi r^2 + \pi r l$ where l is the slant height of the cone. $\pi r l$ is the area of the curved surface of the cone.

The relation between the perpendicular height, h, the slant height, l, and the radius r is that $l^2 = h^2 + r^2$ since the three form a right triangle.

EXAMPLE 1 ....

Find the height of a rectangular based pyramid whose length is one unit more than the width of the base and height is one unit less than twice the length. If the sum of the height, the width and the height is 18, determine the volume and the height of the pyramid.

EXPLANATION

Let the width be x then

Length, $l = x + 1$

Height, $h = 2l - 1 = 2(x + 1) - 1 = 2x + 2 - 1 = 2x + 1$

We are given that $l + w + h = 18$

Upon substitution, we have

$$x + x + 1 + 2x + 1 = 18$$
$$4x + 2 = 18$$
$$4x = 16$$
$$x = 4$$

Width = 4 in

Length = $4 + 1 = 5$ in

Height = $2x + 1 = 2(4) + 1 = 9$ in

$$\text{Volume} = \frac{1}{3} \times lwh = \frac{1}{3} \times 4 \times 5 \times 9 = 4 \times 5 \times 3 = 60 \text{ cubic inches}$$

EXAMPLE 2 ....

The surface area of a cone is 502.7 sq. in. If the radius is 8 in, find the height and the volume of the cone.

EXPLANATION

The surface area is given by $= \pi r^2 + \pi r l = 502.7$

Since $r = 8$

We carry out substitution

$$(\pi \times 8^2) + (\pi \times 8 \times l) = 502.7$$

Upon simplification, we have

$$201.1 + 25.14l = 502.7$$
$$25.14l = 301.6$$
$$l = 12$$

The slant height, l, the perpendicular height, h and the radius r forms a right angle triangle where l is the hypotenuse. By Pythagorean Theorem, we have

$$h = \sqrt{l^2 + r^2} = \sqrt{12^2 + 8^2} = \sqrt{208} = 14.42 \text{ in}$$

$$\text{Volume} = \frac{1}{3}\pi r^2 h = \frac{1}{3}\pi \times 8^2 \times 14.42 = 966.6 \text{ cubic in}$$

GEOMETRIC FORMULAS: VOLUME AND SURFACE AREA OF SPHERES

A sphere is a three dimensional object inform of a ball. The volume of a sphere is given by $\frac{4}{3}\pi r^3$ while its surface area $= 4\pi r^2$.

EXAMPLE 1 ....

Find the surface area and volume of a sphere of radius 3 in.

EXPLANATION

$$\text{Surface area} = 4\pi r^2 = 4 \times \pi \times 3^2 = 113.1 \text{ sq. in}$$

$$\text{Volume} = \frac{4}{3}\pi r^3 = \frac{4}{3} \times \pi \times 3^3 = 113.1 \text{ cubic inches}$$

EXAMPLE 2..

The surface area of a sphere is 94.25 sq. in. Determine its volume.

EXPLANATION

Surface area $= 4\pi r^2 = 94.25$

Upon substitution and simplifying further, we have

$$r^2 = \frac{94.25}{4\pi} = \frac{94.25}{4 \times 3.142} = 7.5 \text{ in}$$

EXAMPLE 3..

While playing, a student hit a ball which fell in water. If a third of the ball was wet, find the area of the ball that was dry if the ball had a diameter of 19 in.

EXPLANATION

Diameter = 19 in hence the radius = 9.5 in

Since $\frac{1}{3}$ of the ball was wet, $1-\frac{1}{3}=\frac{2}{3}$ was dry.

We therefore find the surface area of $\frac{2}{3}$ of the ball.

$$\text{The dry surface} = \frac{2}{3}\times 4\pi r^2 = \frac{2}{3}\times 4\times \pi \times 9.5^2 = 756.1 \text{ sq. in}$$

SURFACE AREA AND VOLUME OF COMPOSITE 3-D GEOMETRIC FIGURES

Composite three dimensional figures are figures that are composed of more than one basic 3 dimensional figure. For instance, it may be composed of a cylinder and a cone, a prism and a cube and so on.

To determine their volume, we divide the figure into known three dimensional figures, find the area of the each figure and add them.

To determine their surface area, we add the areas of the external faces of the figure.

EXAMPLE 1 ....

A toy is composed of a cylinder and a cone on its top. The radius of the cylinder is 5 in while its height is 9 in. Find the surface area of the toy if it is 16 in tall.

EXPLANATION

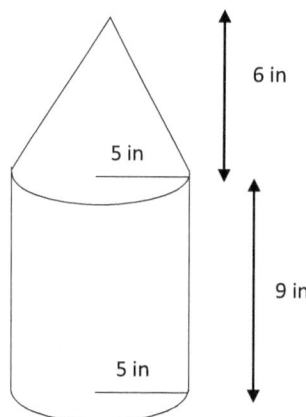

Volume = volume of the cone + volume of the cylinder

$$= \frac{1}{3}\pi r^2 h + \pi r^2 H = \left(\frac{1}{3} \times \pi \times 5^2 \times 6\right) + (\pi \times 5^2 \times 9) = 157.1 + 706.9 = 864 \text{ cubic inches}$$

EXAMPLE 2

Find the volume and the surface area of the figure below.

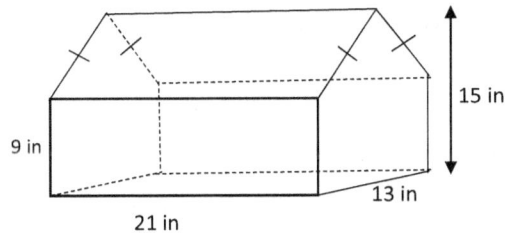

15 in

9 in

13 in

21 in

EXPLANATION

The figure above is composed of two figures, a rectangular prism of length 21 in, width 13 in and height 8 in and a triangular prims whose base is a triangle measuring 13 in base and $15 - 9 = 6$ in. height.

The volume = volume of the rectangular prism + volume of triangular prism

$$= lwh + \frac{1}{2}bhl$$

$$= \left(21 \times 13 \times 9\right) + \left(\frac{1}{2} \times 6 \times 13 \times 21\right)$$

$$= 2457 + 819$$

$$= 3276 \text{ sq. in}$$

Surface area = Sum of external surfaces.

The rectangular prism has five external faces only, one 21 by 13, two 9 by 13 and two 21 by 9. The total surface area of these five surfaces

$$= (21 \times 13) + 2(9 \times 13) + 2(21 \times 9)$$

$$= 273 + 234 + 378$$

$$= 885 \text{ sq. in}$$

The triangular prism has 4 external faces, two equal rectangles and two equal triangles of height 6 in and base 13 in.

We determine the side of the width of the two rectangles of the triangular prism.

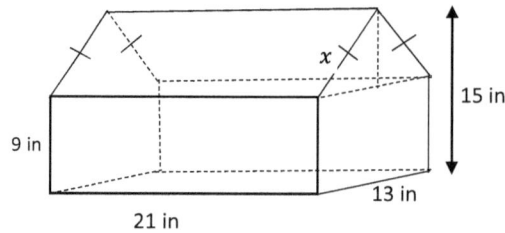

x the height of the triangle = 6 in and half its base = 6.5 in makes a right angle triangle where x is the hypotenuse.

$$x = \sqrt{6.5^2 + 6^2} = \sqrt{78.25} = 8.846 \text{ in}$$

We therefore find the area of two 21 in by 8.846 in rectangles and the two triangles.

$$\text{The surface area of these surfaces} = 2(21 \times 8.846) + 2\left(\frac{1}{2} \times 8.846 \times 13\right)$$

$$= 371.5 + 115$$

$$= 486.5 \text{ sq. in}$$

Total surface area of the solid = 885 + 486.5 = 1371.5 sq. in

RATES, RATIOS, AND PROPORTIONS

The rate is a comparison between two items that have different features. In most cases, we use the unit rate where the first item is compared to the unit of the second item. Example 10 meters per second is a unit rate where a distance of 10 meter is said to have covered within one second.

When two or more items of the same features are compared, we say the comparison is a ratio. For instance, ratio of the number of books to that of pens bought being 3 : 4 or $\frac{3}{4}$ or 3 to 4 implies, in every 3 books bought, 4 pens were also bought.

Proportion is an equation of two rates. If $a : b$ and $p : q$ are equated, we have the equation

$$\frac{a}{b} = \frac{p}{q}$$

Which is equivalent to $aq = bp$.

The numbers a and q are called the extremes and b and p called the means.

There are two main types of proportion, direct proportion and inverse (indirect proportion). Two items a and b are directly proportional if $a = rb$ where r is a constant called constant of proportionality, that is, an increase in one item leads to an increase in the other. Items a and b are inversely proportional if

$$a = \frac{t}{b}$$

where t is the constant of proportionality. That is the increase in one items leads to a decrease of the other.

EXAMPLE 1 ....

A pipe supplier 20 gallons of water in 4 hours. Determine the unit rate of supply.

EXPLANATION

$$\text{The unit rate} = \frac{20}{4} \text{ gallons per hour}$$

$$= 5 \text{ gallons per hour}$$

EXAMPLE 2 ....

There are 24 soccer players and 15 volleyball players in a school. Find the ratio of volleyball to that of soccer players. In a group of 22 players, how many soccer players do we expect to have?

EXPLANATION

The number of volleyball players is 15

The number of soccer players is 24

$$\text{The required ratio} = 15 : 24 = \frac{15}{24} = 5/6$$

The required ratio is 5 : 6

The total ratio is $= 5 + 6 = 11$

The fraction of soccer players $= \frac{6}{11}$

The number of soccer players in the a group of 22 is

$$\frac{6}{11} \times 22 = 6 \times 2 = 12 \text{ players}$$

EXAMPLE 3...

Find the value of x if $\dfrac{4}{x} = \dfrac{28}{70}$

EXPLANATION

We cross multiply to get

$$28x = 280;$$

$$x = \frac{280}{28} = 10$$

Thus $x = 10$

EXAMPLE 4...

The price of 3 pizza is \$63. Alice has 100, how much is she required to add so that she can buy 5 pizzas?

EXPLANATION

We come up with a formula showing this

Let p and s represent pizza and price respectively.

Since increase in the number of pizza implies increase in total cost, the two items are directly proportional, hence we have $s = rp$, where r is a constant of proportionality

When $s = 63$, $p = 3$ upon substitution, we have $63 = 3r$

Thus

$$r = \frac{63}{3} = 21$$

Thus the formula is $s = 21p$.

To buy 5 pizzas, she need $s = 21 \times 5 = \$105$

Since she has \$100, she requires \$105 − \$100 = \$5

WRAPPING IT UP

In this section, we have looked at measurement of various figures. We began with perimeter and area of plane figures and composite plane figures. We have proceeded to look at volume and surface area of three dimensional objects such as prisms, pyramids, spheres and composite three dimensional figures. Finally, we have looked at a form of comparing number referred to as rate, ratio and proportionality.

PROPORTIONALITY, STATISTICS AND PROBABILITY

What You Need to Know About This Section?

In this section, we are going to learn about unit rates and scale drawing which is a special case of rate. We will then proceed to discuss about some of the common methods of representing and analyzing data. It will also be important to familiarize ourselves with permutations and combinations which are widely applied in probability. We will then look at probability then finalize with representations of proportionality and the related equations.

MATH TOPICS

- Compute unit rates. Examples include but are not limited to: unit pricing, constant speed, persons per square mile, BTUs per cubic foot. (Reference 1.21).
- Use scale factors to determine the magnitude of a size change. Convert between actual drawings and scale drawings (Reference 1.22).
- Represent, display, and interpret categorical data in bar graphs or circle graphs (Reference 1.23).
- Represent, display, and interpret data involving one variable plots on the real number line including dot plots, histograms, and box plots (Reference 1.24).
- Represent, display, and interpret data involving two variables in tables and the coordinate plane including scatter plots and graphs (Reference 1.25).
- Calculate the mean, median, mode, and range. Calculate a missing data value, given the average and all the missing data vales but one, as well as calculating the average, given the frequency counts of all the data values, and calculating a weighted average. (Reference 1.26).
- Use counting techniques to solve problems and determine combinations and permutations (Reference 1.27).
- Determine the probability of simple and compound events (Reference 1.28).

MATH TOPICS (contd.)

✍ Solve real-world problems involving linear equations (Reference 1.29).

✍ Compare two different proportional relationships represented in different ways. Examples include but are not limited to: compare a distance-time graph to a distance-time equation to determine which of two moving objects has a greater speed. (Reference 1.30).

INTRODUCTION

In day to day life we usual meat a number of cases on rates. For instance, we express motion of motors in terms of speed which is a unit rate. We use maps to be able to move from one place to unknown place. This possible when we use ratios to convert measurements on maps to the ground. These ratios are called scales. Apart from ratios and rates, we also encounter data. For instance, we could find out the age groups in a given class. To analyses and represent this information, we require the concept of graphs and a discussion of measures such as measures of central tendency. Finally, we are used to prediction of future activities and events. However, this is not accurate if we do not have a standard way of measuring the certainty of these events. This way is referred to as probability. In this section, we are going to look at some of the cases mentions in this introduction along with others.

UNIT RATES

Rate refers to a comparison between two items that have different features. For instance we can compare the number of acres of land a tractor can plow and the number of hours it takes to plow that particular piece of land. If the tractor takes 3 hours to plow 6 acres of land then the rate of plowing is 6 acres in 3 hours or $\frac{6}{3}$ acres per hour. When the second item being compared with, or the denominator of the rate is a unit, (1) then the rate is called a unit rate. For the above case, the unit rate is 2 acres per hour.

EXAMPLE 1

A price of 6 pounds of sugar is $1.08. What would be the cost of a unit pound of sugar?

EXPLANATION

The unit cost would be the unit rate

$$\$\frac{1.08}{6} \text{per pound}$$

$$\$\frac{1.08}{6} \text{per pound} = \$0.18 \text{ per pound}$$

EXAMPLE 2...

A car covers a total of 248 miles in four hours. Determine the unit rate of its motion.

EXPLANATION

Unit rate = rate of motion (speed) = 248 miles divided by 4 hours

$$= \frac{248}{4} = 62 \text{ mi/hr}$$

EXAMPLE 3...

A survey was done to establish the number of households in a given square mile in a suburb of a city. It was found that 500000 people leave within 8 square miles. Determine the population in unit square mile.

EXPLANATION

$$\text{Unit rate} = \frac{500000}{8} \text{ people per square mile}$$

$$= 62500 \text{ poeple per square mile}$$

SCALE FACTORS AND SCALE DRAWINGS

A scale factor is a ratio comparing two measurements. In most cases, we compare length, area, volume, density among others. A scale factor comparing two lengths is called a linear scale factor, those comparing two area is called area scale factor and those comparing two volumes is called volume scale factor. Items whose characteristics can be describing using scale factors of corresponding lengths (sides) are said to be similar.

$$\text{Scale factor} = \frac{\text{Measurement of the new item}}{\text{Measurement of the original item}}$$

If the triangle is increased so that its original base is 8 in and its new base is 12 in, then the linear scale factor will be

$$\text{linear scale factor} = \frac{\text{Base of the original triangle}}{\text{Base of the new triangle}} = \frac{12}{8} = 1.5$$

The area scale factor is a scale factor that compare the length.

$$\text{Area scale factor} = (\text{linear scale factor})^2$$

$$\text{Volume scale factor} = (\text{Linear scale factor})^3$$

A special case of a linear scale factor is the scale. A scale is a ratio comparing two lengths where (in most cases), the first length is given as one unit. A scale is a ratio that is used in the building industry to compare the transfer the length of the maps of building to the actual building on the ground. A part from the building industry, it is also used in survey of places, engineering field among others. To build something, a small proportional drawing is made with accurate measurements. If the length of this item is 9 in and the length of the actual items is supposed to be 90, 000 then the scale factor is

$$9 \text{ to } 90,000 \text{ or } \frac{9}{90,000} = \frac{1}{10,000} \text{ or } 1 : 10,000.$$

The scale, $1 : 10,000$ or $\frac{1}{10,000}$ or 1 to 10,000 means that 1 unit (inch for this case) on the map is equivalent to 10,000 units (inches) on the actual ground. This scale can be used to determine the equivalent ground measurements of the item from the map measurements.

EXAMPLE 1 ....

The lengths of two similar rectangles are 15 in and 12 in respectively. If the width of the smaller rectangle is 8 in, find the area of the smaller rectangle.

EXPLANATION

$$\text{Linear scale factor} = \frac{\text{Length of the bigger rectangle}}{\text{Length of smaller rectangle}} = \frac{15}{12} = \frac{5}{4}$$

Since the two figures are similar, we have

$$\frac{\text{Width of the bigger rectangle}}{\text{Width of smaller rectangle}} = \frac{5}{4}$$

iGlobal GED Math Study Guide

$$\frac{x}{8} = \frac{5}{4}$$
$$4x = 8 \times 5$$
$$x = \frac{8 \times 5}{4} = 10 \text{ in}$$

EXAMPLE 2...

The length of a piece of land is that is inform of a square is 6 miles. If the map of this land is drawn using a scale factor of 1 : 126,720, find the area of map of the piece of land.

EXPLANATION

The scale is 1 : 126,720 implying 1 in represents 126,720 in.

We know that 1 mile = 63360 in

Hence   6 miles = 6\times63360 = 380160 in

If 126 720 in is represented by 1 in

380 160 in will be represented by

$$\frac{380160 \times 1}{126720} = 3 \text{ in}$$

Thus the side of the square map is 3 in.

Its area will be $3^2 = 9$ sq. in

BAR GRAPHS AND CIRCLE GRAPHS

A bar graph is a graph that is composed of bars whose heights are proportional to the frequency of items in data. They bars may be horizontal or vertical. Bar graphs are used in situations where one need to make comparisons among the items plotted or in situations here one needs to show a trend of events for some time.

Circle graph is a circular representation of data where data items take proportional shapes of the circle. The proportions expressed in terms of angles or percentage. Circle graphs are used when one is interested in knowing the fraction an item represents. It is also used to show comparison.

EXAMPLE 1 ....

A survey was conducted to establish the favorite fruit that students like. The table below shows the results.

Fruit	Apples	Bananas	Grapes	Guavas	Oranges
Number of students	21	18	26	13	17

Draw a graph showing the graph.

EXPLANATION

We will create a bar graph with vertical bars. The scale showing the numbers of students will be on the vertical axis and the type of fruits on the horizontal axis. Upon plotting, we have the following graph.

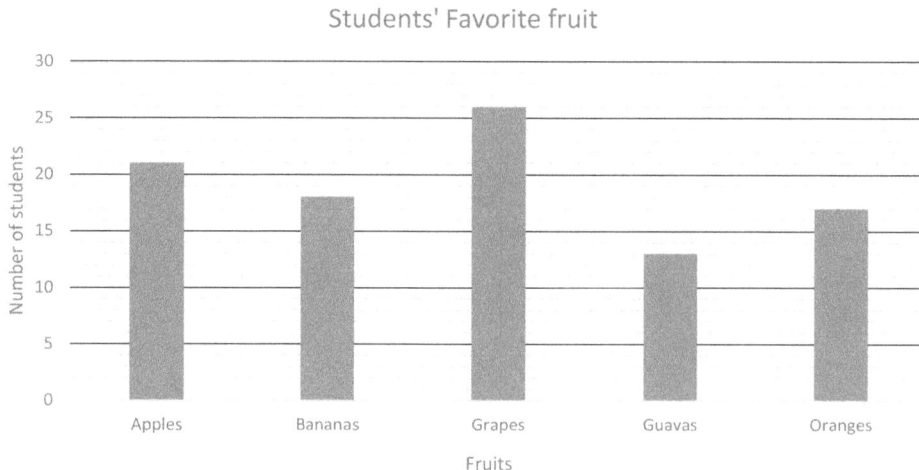

EXAMPLE 2..

The graph below shows the Christopher's budget for the month of October 2015.

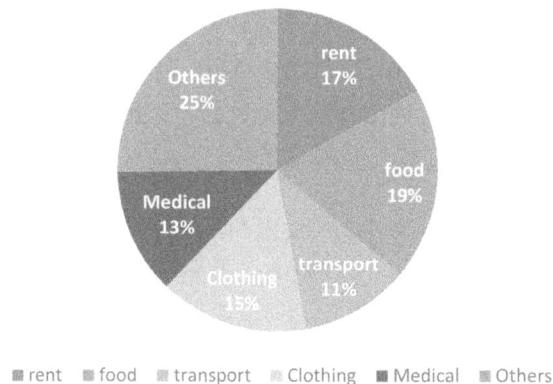

iGlobal GED Math Study Guide

If she spent $180 on clothing, find out

(i). His total budget

(ii). The amount spent on transport more than that spent on rent.

EXPLANATION

(i). The percentage of clothing is 15%

Since 100% is the whole proportion implying the whole budget, we have the comparison statement

15% implies $180

100% will imply

$$\frac{100}{15} \times 180 = \$1200$$

Total budget is $1200

(ii). Amount spent on transport = 11%

Amount spent on rent = 17%

The difference = 17% − 11% = 6%

6% is equivalent to

$$\frac{6}{100} \times 1200 = \$72$$

DOT PLOTS, HISTOGRAMS, AND BOX PLOTS

Dot plots is a kind of graphical representation where frequency is represented by the number of dots. Sometimes, a key may be given so that a dot represents more than one unit.

Histogram is a graph that is composed on bars that are in contact with each other and whose height is proportional to the frequency of the items represented. They used in representing continuous data.

Box plot is a graphical representations inform of a box where the end of the box represents the lower and upper quarter while a line inside the box represents the median of the data. The box plot is used to show how data values are distributed around the median.

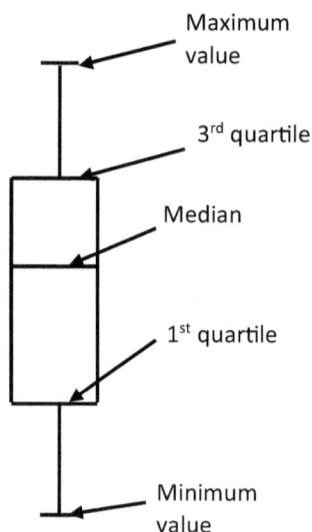

The median is a value whose position divides the data into two equal sections when data is arranged in ascending or descending order. The median of the first half is called the first quartile while the median of the second half is called the third quartile.

EXAMPLE 1 ....

The data below shows the height of students in feet.

$$4.5, 5.6, 3.5, 5.4, 5.3, 4.6, 4.3, 3.9, 4.5, 5.1, 4.3, 4.9, 4.0$$

Construct a box plot for the data.

EXPLANATION

We arrange the data in ascending order

$$3.5, 3.9, 4.0, 4.3, 4.3, 4.5, 4.5, 4.6, 4.9, 5.1, 5.3, 5.4, 5.6$$

The data 13 data values

The median number is in the 7th position, that is, 4.5

The first half is 3.5, 3.9, 4.0, 4.3, 4.3, 4.5 whose median is the average of 4.0 and 4.3

$$\text{First quartile} = \frac{4.0 + 4.3}{2} = \frac{8.3}{2} = 4.15$$

The second half is 4.6, 4.9, 5.1, 5.3, 5.4, 5.6 whose median is the average of 5.1 and 5.3

$$\text{The third quartile} = \frac{5.1 + 5.3}{2} = \frac{10.4}{2} = 5.2$$

Maximum value = 5.6

Minimum value = 3.2

Upon drawing the box plot, we have

–5
–4
–3
–2
–1

EXAMPLE 2...

The graph below shows the number of times a given number of students visits a swimming pool every day.

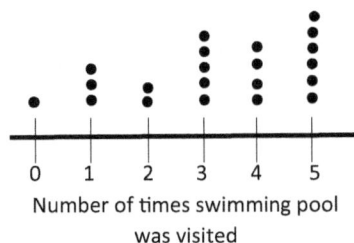

Number of times swimming pool
was visited

Find the

The number of students visits the swimming pool more than 3 times a week

The number of students that visits the swimming pool

EXPLANATION

From the graph, one person did not make any visit to the pool

Three students visited once a week

Two students visited twice a week and so on

The number of students that visited more than three times implies those that visited four times and five times.

Four students visited 4 times and five students visit 6 times

The required answer is $4 + 6 = 10$

The number of students that visited the pool is the sum of those that visited once, twice up to five times. That is $3 + 2 + 5 + 4 + 6 = 20$

EXAMPLE 3...

The table below shows the performance of students in a test. Draw a histogram showing the results.

Marks	41 – 50	51 – 60	61 – 70	71 – 80	81 – 90	91 – 100
Number of students	2	4	9	12	4	5

EXPLANATION

We determine the class boundaries, that is 0.5 less or more than the lower class limits (the bounds of the classes as given in the table)

The class boundaries are 40.5, 50.5, 60.5, 70.5, 80.5, 90.5, 100.5

It can be seen that the classes will be between any two values above

Upon plotting, we have the following graph

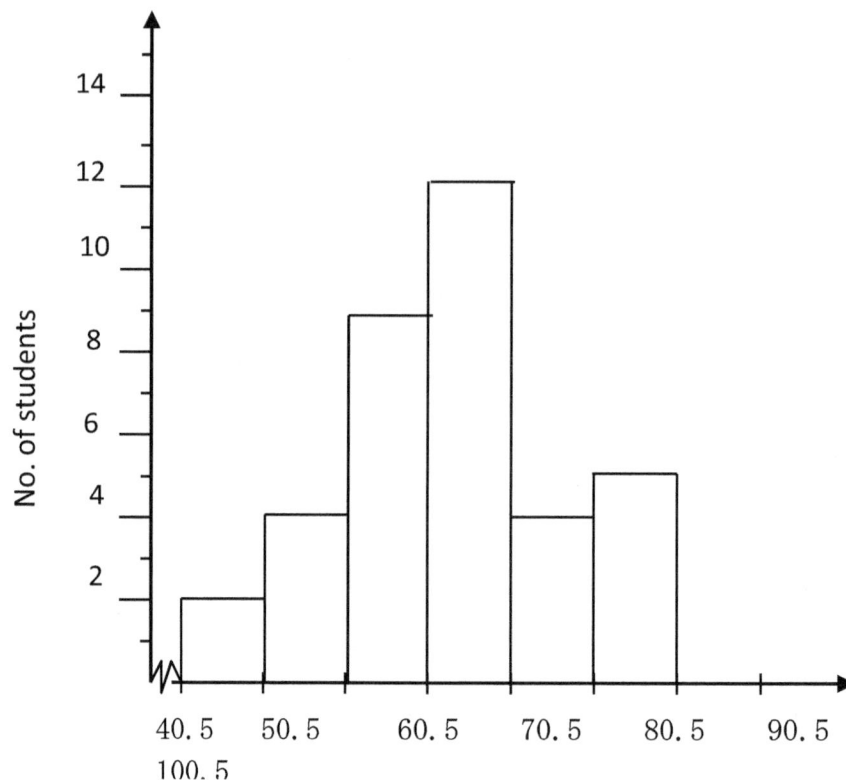

SCATTER PLOTS AND GRAPHS

In some case, data may be based on two items or variables that may be or may not be related. For instance, a survey mat be done to establish the amount monthly average rain for the whole year and the average monthly humidity y in the area. Since these two variables are related, their relation can be established when plotted as a pair of coordinates of a point to come up with a line graph. Such line graphs showing the trend of two variables that are related is called scatter graph while a series of points from the graph is drawn is called the scatter plot.

The scatter plot we may draw a line that is closest to most points on the graph. This line is called the line of the best fit. The line of the best fit may be linear, quadratic, exponential graphs and so on. We are most interested in line graph.

When the line of the best fit slopes to the right, we say it has negative slope hence the variables are negatively correlated. When it slopes to the left, we say the line is positively correlated. When the all or almost all points fall on the line, we say the variables are strongly correlated, when most point lie on or closer to the line, the variables are moderately correlated and when they are very far from the line, the variables are weakly correlated. A correlation does not exists in the points are uniformly distributed all over in the plot area.

EXAMPLE 1 ....

Identify the kind of correlation in the graph below

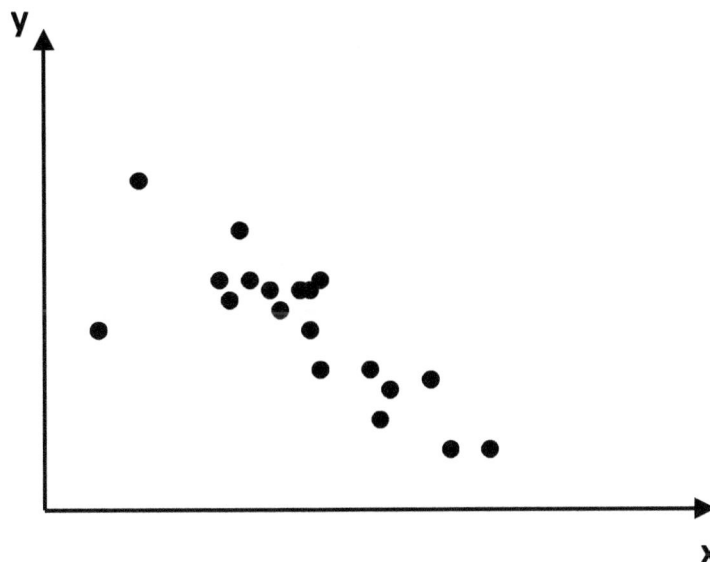

EXPLANATION

We try to get the line of the best fit

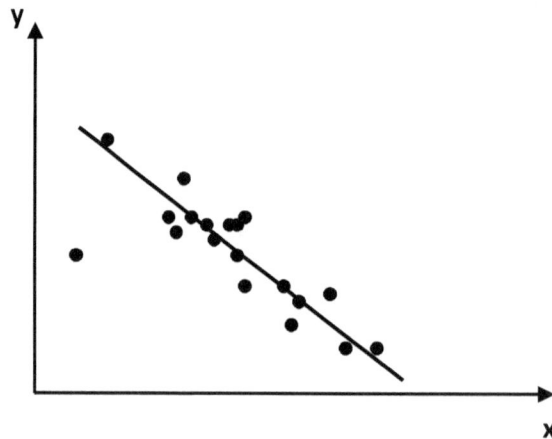

Te line of the best fit slopes to the right. Furthermore, most points are closer to the line of the best fit, hence the two variables have a strong negative correlation.

EXAMPLE 2..

The table below shows the data on the number of hours students spend reading a day and their performance. Draw a scatter plot and identify the kind of relation between the two variables.

Hours read	1	1	1.5	2	2	2.5	2.5	2.5	3	3.5	4	4.5	4.5	4	5	5
Performance (%)	65	64	70	52	53	59	73	74	65	68	83	80	74	76	68	76

EXPLANATION

We plot the Performance against the number of hours read and draw the line of the best fit.

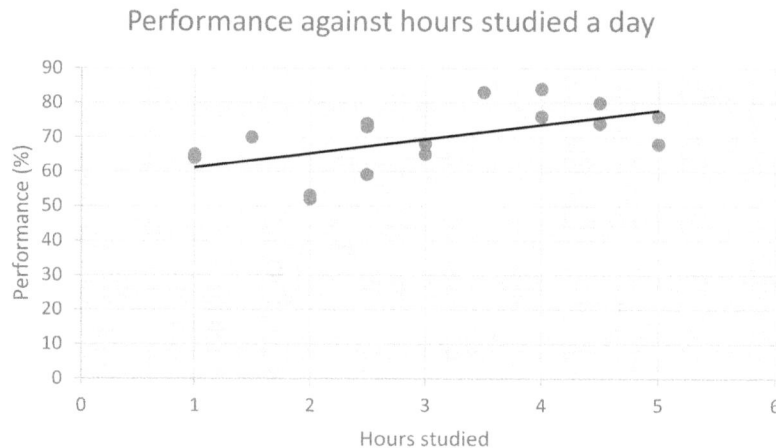

Performance against hours studied a day

iGlobal GED Math Study Guide

The line of the best fit slopes to the left and most of the points a a bit far from the line however, there are within a certain distance from the line, hence, the two variables have a moderate positive correlation.

MEASURES OF CENTRAL TENDENCY

Measures of central tendency refers to the values of a given data that try to locate the center of the data, hence they are used as single representatives of a given data. These measures are mean, median and mode.

Mean refers to the sum of values divided by the number of these values. Median is the middle value of the data when arranged in either ascending or descending order. Mode is the most common value in data. We will also look at range which is the difference between the largest and smallest value of the data.

EXAMPLE 1 ....

The mean of 14 numbers is 12. If the other thirteen numbers are 12, 13, 13.5, 12.1, 11, 13.5, 12.1, 11.8, 11.5, 11.5, 11, 11.7 and 12, find the other number.

Let the missing number be x, then the mean is

$$\frac{12+13+13.5+12.1+11+13.5+12.1+11.8+11.5+11.5+11+11.7+12+x}{14}=12$$

$$\frac{156.7+x}{14}=12$$

$$156.7+x=168$$

$$x=11.3$$

EXAMPLE 2...

The table below shows the age of students in grade 10.

Age	Number of students
15	3
16	13
17	12
18	5
19	1

Find

(i). The mode of the data

(ii). The average age of the students

(iii). The range of the data.

EXPLANATION

(i). The mode is the most common value. From the table, there are 13 students with an age of 16. There is no age with more than 13 students. Hence the mode is 16.

(ii). The average is the sum divided by the number

Since some ages appear more than once, we will be multiplying by the number of the students to get the total age

$$\text{Total age} = (15 \times 3) + (16 \times 13) + (17 \times 12) + (18 \times 5) + (19 \times 1) = 566$$

Total number of students = 3 + 13 + 12 + 5 + 1 = 34

$$\text{The mean} = \frac{566}{34} = 16.65 \text{ years}$$

(iii). The highest age = 19 and the lowest value = 15

$$\text{The range} = 19 - 15 = 4$$

PROBABILITY: COMBINATIONS AND PERMUTATIONS

Permutation refers to the arrangement of items where order is required. For instance, in permutation of five items where two items (say M and A) should be next to each other MATH and AMTH are two different arrangements since M begins in one arrangement and A in the other.

Combination is an arrangement of items where order is not necessary. In the above example, MATH and AMTH are the same since A and M are next to each other and the order A first then M or M first then A is not necessary. We use this concept to count the number of times a certain number of item(s) can be selected or arranged.

The permutation of n number of items without replacement is

$$n! = n(n-1)(n-2)(n-3)\ldots 4.3.2.1$$

If $n = 5$, then the number of arrangement of 5 items is $5! = 5 \times 4 \times 3 \times 2 \times 1 = 120$

By definition, $1! = 0! = 1$

The permutation of n items taking r at a time is

$$nPr = \frac{n!}{(n-r)!}$$

The combination of n items taking r at a time is

$$nCr = \binom{n}{r} = \frac{n!}{r!(n-r)!}$$

EXAMPLE 1 ....

Solve $6C5$ and $8P3$

EXPLANATION

$$6C5 = \frac{6!}{5!(6-5)!} = \frac{6!}{5! \times 1!} = \frac{6 \times 5!}{5!} = 6$$

Since $6! = 6 \times 5!$

$$8P3 = \frac{8!}{3!(8-3)!} = \frac{8!}{3! \times 5!} \quad \text{we have}$$

Since $8! = 8 \times 7 \times 6 \times 5!$

$$\frac{8!}{3! \times 5!} = \frac{8 \times 7 \times 6 \times 5!}{3 \times 2 \times 1 \times 5!} = 8 \times 7 = 56$$

EXAMPLE 2..

If four people are to sit around a table, how many arrangements can there be if two have to sit next to each other.

EXPLANATION

Total number of people = 4

Number of people to sit together = 2

Here order is not required as long as the two site together, thus, this is a combination problem

$$4C2 = \frac{4!}{2!(4-2)!} = \frac{4!}{2! \times 2!} = \frac{4 \times 3 \times 2 \times 1}{2 \times 2} = 6$$

EXAMPLE 3..

I teacher is required to select 10 students from a grade 3 and 4 classes to attend a state education function. If grade 3 has 12 students and grade 4 has 15 students

(i). How many way can the teacher select 10 students from the two classes?

(ii). How many ways can they select 4 students from grade 3 and 6 from grade 3

EXPLANATION

(i). Selecting 10 students from the two classes does not require any order, hence any order is not required. The total number of students $= 12 + 15 = 27$

The problem is

$$27C10 = \frac{27!}{10!(27-10)!} = \frac{27!}{10! \times 17!}$$

$$10! = 3,628,800$$

$$\frac{27!}{10! \times 17!} = \frac{27 \times 26 \times 25 \times 24 \times 23 \times 22 \times 21 \times 20 \times 19 \times 18 \times 17!}{3628800 \times 17!}$$

$$= \frac{27 \times 26 \times 25 \times 24 \times 23 \times 22 \times 21 \times 20 \times 19 \times 18}{3628800}$$

$$= 8436285$$

(ii). We select 4 from a group of 12 and 6 from a group of 15

Thus, we have $12C4 \times 15C6$

$$12C4 \times 15C6 = \frac{12}{4! \times (12-4)!} \times \frac{15!}{6! \times (15-6)!}$$

$$= \frac{12!}{4! \times 8!} \times \frac{15!}{6! \times 9!}$$

$$= \frac{12 \times 11 \times 10 \times 9 \times 8!}{4! \times 8!} \times \frac{15 \times 14 \times 13 \times 12 \times 11 \times 10 \times 9!}{6! \times 9!}$$

$$= \frac{12 \times 11 \times 10 \times 9}{4!} \times \frac{15 \times 14 \times 13 \times 12 \times 11 \times 10}{6!}$$

$$= \frac{12 \times 11 \times 10 \times 9}{24} \times \frac{15 \times 14 \times 13 \times 12 \times 11 \times 10}{720} = 99 \times 5 \times 35 \times 143 = 2477475$$

PROBABILITY: SIMPLE AND COMPOUND EVENTS

Probability is a measure of how certain an event is likely to occur. The probability of an event is a fraction whose numerator is the number of favorable outcomes of an event and denominator is the total possible outcomes of an event. The total probability is 1. When the probability is zero then event A will not occur. When the probability is closer to 1, then the event is likely to occur. When it is closer to zero, the event is not likely to occur.

For instance, A coin has two faces, when tossed, we expect a head or a coin.

Thus, the total outcome is 2. Since we expect only a head, the probability of getting a head, H, is

$$P(H) = \frac{1}{2}.$$

This is case of a simple event, that is when we are considering one item.

If $P(H)$ is the probability that an event occurs, then the probability that the event does not occur is

$$P\left(H^c\right) = 1 - P(H)$$

For the case of compound events, we consider more than one item.

If A and B are two events, the probability of success of A and B (probability of A and B occurring) is

$$P(A \text{ and } B) = P(A)P(B)$$

The probability of A or B (or B or A occurring) is

$$P(A \text{ and } B) = P(A) + P(B)$$

EXAMPLE 1 ....

If a die is rolled once, what is the probability that

(i). A five appears

(ii). A number more than 2 appears

EXPLANATION

(i). A die has six sides. When it is tossed, we expect only one face having no. 5

Hence the favorable outcomes = 1

The total possible outcomes = 6

$$P(5) = \frac{\text{Favourable outcomes}}{\text{Total possible outcomes}} = \frac{1}{6}$$

(ii). The numbers more than 2 are 3, 4, 5 and 6. Thus, the favorable outcomes = 4

The total possible outcomes = 6

$$P(\text{Number more than 2}) = \frac{4}{6} = \frac{2}{3}$$

EXAMPLE 2...

If a coin and a die are tossed and rolled once respectively, what is the probability that

(i). A tail and a three appears

(ii). A head or a six appears

EXPLANATION

(i). When a coin is tossed, we expect a head or a tail hence the probability of occurrence of a tail is

$$P(T) = \frac{\text{Number of tails}}{\text{Total possible outcomes}} = \frac{1}{2}$$

A die has faces with one faced labelled three. Hence the probability of getting a three is

$$P(3) = \frac{1}{6}$$

$$P(T \text{ and } 3) = P(T) \times P(3) = \frac{1}{2} \times \frac{1}{6}$$

$$= \frac{1}{12}$$

(ii). When a coin is tossed, we expect a head or a tail hence the probability of occurrence of a head is

$$P(H) = \frac{\text{Number of heads}}{\text{Total possible outcomes}} = \frac{1}{2}$$

A die has faces with one faced labelled six. Hence the probability of getting a six is

$$P(6) = \frac{1}{6}$$

$$P(H \text{ or } 6) = P(H) + P(6) = \frac{1}{2} + \frac{1}{6}$$

$$= \frac{3+1}{6}$$

$$= \frac{4}{6}$$

$$= \frac{2}{3}$$

EXAMPLE 3...

A bag has 3 red balls, 4 yellow balls and 5 blue balls. If two balls are drawn at random, what is the probability that

(i). Both of them are yellow

(ii). One is a red and another is a blue ball.

EXPLANATION

When a ball is picked, we expect it to be a red, a yellow or a blue

After picking a red ball, we can pick a red, a yellow or a blue ball

After picking a yellow ball, we can pick a red, a yellow or a blue ball

After picking a blue ball, we can pick a red, a yellow or a blue ball

Hence, we have a tree diagram

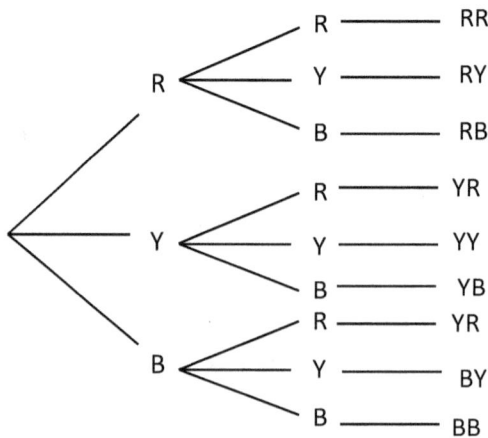

From the diagram above, the all possible outcomes are RR, RY, RB, YR, YY, YB, YR, BY and BB

(i). Total number of balls is 12

Both are yellow implies YY,

Y in the first trial and Y in the second trial.

Probability of picking a yellow ball in the first trial is $\dfrac{4}{12} = \dfrac{1}{3}$

After picking a yellow ball, they remain 3 out of 11

Probability of picking a yellow ball a second time is $\dfrac{3}{11}$

The required probability $= P(YY) = P(Y)P(Y_2) = \dfrac{1}{3} \times \dfrac{3}{11} = \dfrac{1}{11}$

(ii). One is a red and another is a blue ball implies RB or BR

$P(RB) = P(R)P(B_2)$ where $P(B_2)$ implies picking a blue ball in the second trial

$$= \dfrac{3}{12} \times \dfrac{4}{11} = \dfrac{1}{11}$$

$P(BR) = P(B)P(R_2)$ where $P(R_2)$ implies picking a red ball in the second trial

$$= \dfrac{5}{12} \times \dfrac{3}{11} = \dfrac{5}{44}$$

$$P(RB \text{ or } BR) = \dfrac{1}{11} + \dfrac{5}{44} = \dfrac{9}{44}$$

PROBLEM SOLVING WITH LINEAR EQUATIONS

Linear equations refers to an expression in one unknown that is equated to a number. Example $3x + 1 = 2$ is a linear equation where the unknown is x. In this chapter, we are going to look at examples on how to form these linear equations and solve them.

EXAMPLE 1 ......

Twice a number is 4 more than the number 14. What is the number?

EXPLANATION

Let the number be x

Then $$2x = 14 + 4$$

We then solve it

$$2x = 18$$
$$x = 9$$

The number is 9

EXAMPLE 2......

A pizza was bought at $124 after a discount of 15%. What was the initial price of Pizza?

EXPLANATION

Let the initial price be x

$$\text{Final price} = \text{initial price} - \text{discount price}$$

$$\text{Discount} = \frac{15}{100}x$$

We now have the equation

$$x - \frac{15}{100}x = 124$$

$$\frac{85}{100}x = 124$$

$$x = 124 \times \frac{100}{85} = \$145.9$$

EXAMPLE 3...

Jane takes 50 min to drive to her work place. While James 5 minutes less to drive to his work place. If they drive at the same average speed how far is James work place given that James is 12 miles away?

EXPLANATION

Let Jane's distance to the work place be x

Then her speed is

$$\frac{x}{50} \text{ mi/min}$$

James takes $50 - 5 = 45$ min while his distance from the work place is 12. Thus, his speed is

$$\frac{12}{45} \text{ mi/min}$$

Since the speed are equal, we have the equation

$$\frac{x}{50} = \frac{12}{45}$$

Thus. $$x = \frac{12}{45} \times 50 = 13.33 \text{ miles}$$

PROPORTIONAL RELATIONSHIPS REPRESENTATIONS

Proportion refers to a comparison of two items whose value increases as the other decreases or increases. We have two types of proportional relationships; direct and indirect proportion. Direct proportion of two variables x and y is when we have $y = kx$ where k is a constant of proportionality. Indirect proportion is when we have $xy = c$ or $y = \frac{c}{x}$ where c is the constant of proportionality. Our aim to find out if given two proportional representations are equal or not.

EXAMPLE 1 ....

Find out the graphical representation of the relationship $p = 2q$

EXPLANATION

We need to find out a line where when q increased by a unit, p increases by twice the unit and when q is zero p is zero.

Thus, when q = 0, p = 0 and when q = 1, p =2. We draw a line passing through (0,0) and (1,2).

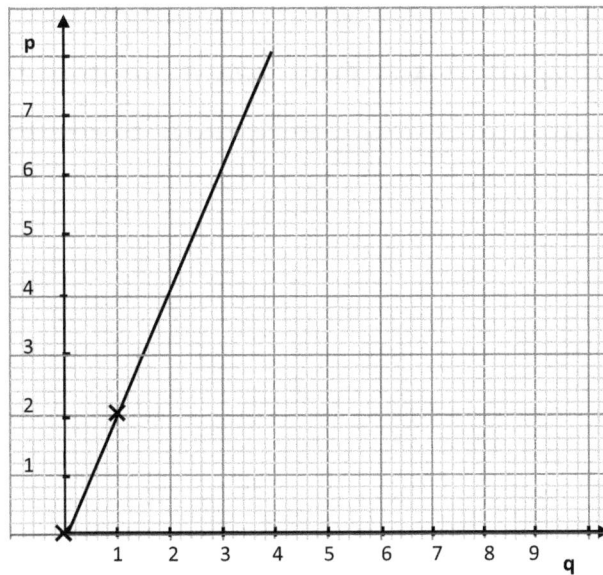

EXAMPLE 2..

Find the proportional relationship of the following table

R	0.8	1	2	4
H	20	16	8	4

EXPLANATION

When R increases, H decreases hence this is an indirect proportional relationship given by

$RH = c$ where c is the constant of proportionality

We find c. $c = 0.8 \times 20 = 1 \times 16 = 16$

Thus, the relation is $H = \dfrac{16}{R}$ OR $HR = 16$

WRAPPING IT UP

In this section, we have looked at rates and a special case of date called scale drawing. Having the idea of scale in mind, we proceeded to look at graphical representation of data which uses the concept of scale a great deal. We have also looked at data analysis using measures of central tendency. We proceeded to look at counting techniques that ushered as into the world of probability. We have completed by looking at linear equations and representation of proportional relations.

ALGEBRAIC FORMULATIONS AND SOLUTIONS

What You Need to Know About This Section?

In this section, we will learn how we can formulate expression and equations and also learn how to solve them. We will go further to compare different representations of functions by identifying if they are similar or not. The expression and equations will be mostly linear and quadratic however, we will also consider some cases where the expressions and equations are more than a quadratic.

MATH TOPICS

- ✍ Compare properties of two linear or quadratic functions each represented in a different way (algebraically, numerically in tables, graphically or by verbal descriptions). Examples include but are not limited to: given a linear function represented by a table of values and a linear function represented by an algebraic expression, determine which function has the greater rate of change (Reference 1.31).
- ✍ Write one-variable and multi-variable linear equations to represent context. (Reference 1.32).
- ✍ Write one-variable quadratic equations to represent context. (Reference 1.33).
- ✍ Add, subtract, factor, multiply and expand linear expressions with rational coefficients (Reference 1.34).
- ✍ Write linear expressions as part of word-to-symbol translations or to represent common settings (Reference 1.35).
- ✍ Add, subtract, multiply polynomials, including multiplying two binomials, or divide factorable polynomials (Reference 1.36).
- ✍ Write polynomials expressions as part of word-to-symbol translations or to represent common settings (Reference 1.37).
- ✍ Add, subtract, multiply, and divide rational expressions. (Reference 1.38).
- ✍ Write rational expressions as part of word-to-symbol translations or to represent common settings (Reference 1.39).
- ✍ Solve a system of two simultaneous linear equations by graphing, substitution, or linear combination. Solve real-word problems leading to a system of linear equations (Reference 1.40).

INTRODUCTION

In day to day life, we meet a number of situations and problems that easily be solved by applying mathematics. For instance, it requires a simple formula to calculate the cost of any number of books of the same price bought. All these requires the use of algebra where an equation is formed solved and interpreted based on the context of the problem. In this content, we learn how to form these expressions, equations, represent them and manipulate them.

COMPARING PROPERTIES OF TWO LINEAR OR QUADRATIC FUNCTIONS

Linear functions are relations whose graphs are straight lines. They are fully described by their slope with y intercept or x intercept, or a slope with both two intercepts. A linear function is given in slope –y-intercept form as $y = mx + c$ where m is the slope of the line, c the y intercept, x and y the independent and dependent variables respectively.

Quadratic functions are relations whose graphs is in form of a curve. The most important features that they have is that their graphs are inform of a parabola, thus having a vertex. Their graph is also symmetrical about a line passing through the vertex. The equation of the quadratic function is generally given as $y = ax^2 + bx + c$ where $a \uparrow 0$, a,b and c are constants. Examples of quadratic functions are $y = 3x^2 + 1$, $y = x^2 + x - 4$. A part from the symmetry and the vertex, the graphs of quadratic functions may have y intercepts and x intercepts (which in most cases are two).

In this section, we are interested to find out if given two different representations of a line or quadratic curve, we may try to figure out if they describe the same or different lines or curves.

EXAMPLE 1 ....

Find out if the table below represents the data generated using the following functions.

(i). $y = 4x - 3$

x	0	3	5	-1	-4	8	-2

y	-3	9	17	7	-19	29	-11

(ii). $y = 2x^2 + 4x + 1$

x	1	-2	4	-3	6	-6	9
y	7	1	49	7	97	49	199

EXPLANATION

We use the equations and find out if we will get the given table using the equation.

(i). $y = 4x - 3$

When $x = 0$, $y = 4(0) - 3 = -3$

        $x = 3$, $y = 4(3) - 3 = 9$

        $x = 5$, $y = 4(5) - 3 = 17$

        $x = -1$, $y = 4(-1) - 3 = -7$

        $x = -4$, $y = 4(-4) - 3 = -19$

        $x = 8$, $y = 4(8) - 3 = 29$

        $x = -2$, $y = 4(-2) - 3 = -11$

From the calculation, we find out that when $x = -1$, $y = -7$ and not 7. Hence the tabular and algebraic representations are of different lines.

(ii). $y = 2x^2 + 4x + 1$

When $x = 1$, $y = 2(1)^2 + 4(1) + 1 = 7$

        $x = -2$, $y = 2(-2)^2 + 4(-2) + 1 = 1$

        $x = 4$, $y = 2(4)^2 + 4(4) + 1 = 49$

        $x = -3$, $y = 2(-3)^2 + 4(-3) + 1 = 7$

        $x = 6$, $y = 2(6)^2 + 4(6) + 1 = 97$

        $x = -6$, $y = 2(-6)^2 + 4(-6) + 1 = 49$

        $x = 9$, $y = 2(9)^2 + 4(9) + 1 = 199$

These values are equivalent to those that are in the table hence the tabular and algebraic representations of the quadratic function of the same curve.

EXAMPLE 2...

Identify an equation whose graph is given by

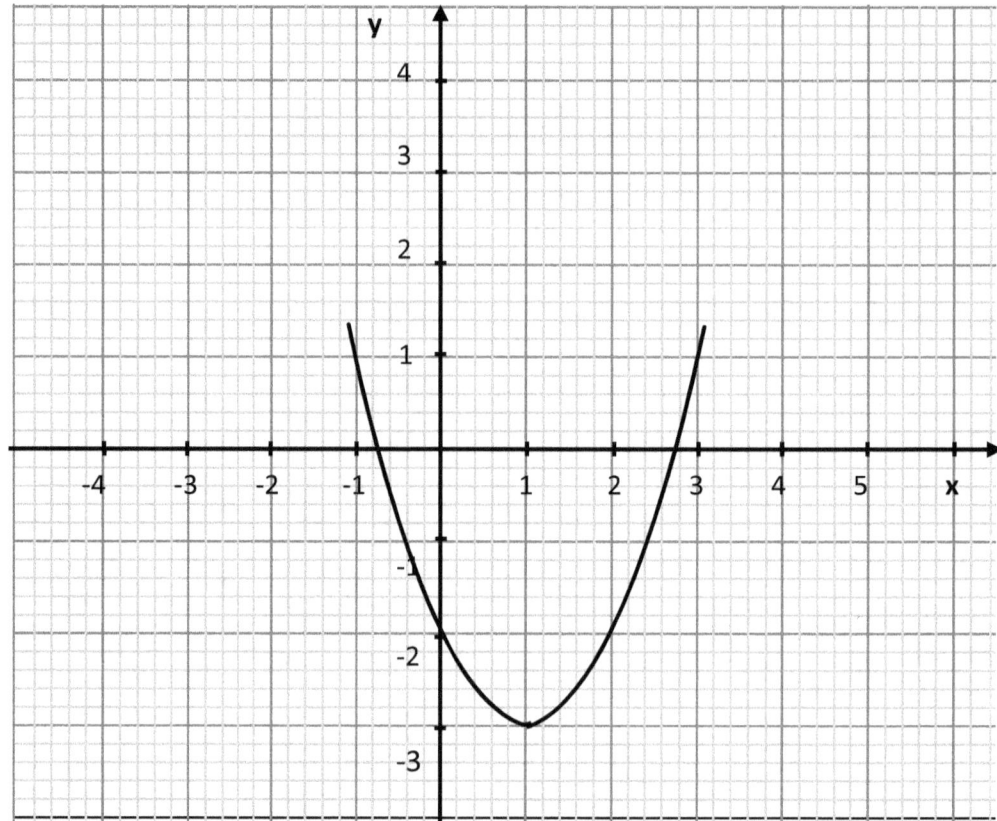

A. $y = x^2 - 2x - 2$

B. $y = x^2 - 2x + 2$

C. $y = x^2 + 2x + 2$

D. $y = x^2 + 2x - 2$

EXPLANATION

From the graph, we can identify the points through which the graph passes. These are

$$(-1,1), (0,-2), (1,-3), (3,1)$$

We use the points to identify an equation that can be satisfied using these equations.

First, point (0,–2) will reduce the equations that we will test.

(0,–2) Implies that when $x = 0$, $y = –2$. Thus, the equation must have a y intercept of –2. From the equations below, we narrow down to $y = x^2 – 2x – 2$ and $y = x^2 + 2x – 2$.

We then use (1,–3) to test the required equation.

When $x = 1$ we have $y = 1^2 + 2 – 2 = 1$

$x = 1$, we have $y = 1^2 – 2 – 2 = –3$

The equation satisfied by at least two points (0,–2) and (1,–3) is only $y = x^2 – 2x – 2$

We therefore proceed to see if the remaining points lie on the graph given by this equation.

$x = –1$, we have $y = (–1)^2 – 2(–1) – 2 = –3$

$x = 3$, we have $y = (3)^2 – 2(3) – 2 = 1$

Thus, the graph above and equation $y = x^2 – 2x – 2$ are representations of the same quadratic function.

EXAMPLE 3...

Find out if the table and the graph below are representations of the same quadratic function.

x	–2	0	2	4
y	0	1	2	3

EXPLANATION

From, the graph above, we can locate four points that lie on the line. These are (0,–2), (0,1), (2,2) and (4,3)

Thus can have table having the x and the corresponding y values as shown below

x	0	1	2	3
y	-2	0	2	4

This table and the table in the equation are not identical since three points don't match. Hence, the table given and the graph are representations of different linear functions.

ONE AND MULTI-VARIABLE LINEAR EQUATIONS

There are day to day problems whose solutions can be determined using equations of one variable or multi-variable linear equations. In this section, we will look at how we can form such equations from a given context.

EXAMPLE 1 ....

After five matches, Little stars soccer club had 5 points. A team gets three points in every win. If after some time, the team has 17 points, write an equation showing the number of matches they played if they won all matches they played after the first five matches.

EXPLANATION

The initial amount of points (after 5 matches) = 5

After one win, the club gets 3 points

After the second win, the club gets (2 × 3) points $(2 \times 3)\,points$

Let the total number of wins be x.

Then after ξ wins, the points earned will be $3x$

The total number of points will be $5 + 3x = 17$

The required equation is $5 + 3x = 17$

EXAMPLE 2...

Jolly is 2 years more than three times the age of his son. In 6 years to come, the sum of their age will be 54. Write an equation showing their total age 2 years to come.

EXPLANATION

Let the age of the son be x, three times this age is $3x$

Jolly's age $= 3x + 2$

In 6 years, each ones age will increase by 6 hence, we have

Son age in 6 year $= x + 6$

Jolly's age in 6 years $= 3x + 2 + 6 = 3x + 8$

The sum of the age in 6 years $= 3x + 8 + x + 6 = 54$

In two years to come, that is 4 years before the 6 years, their age will be 4 less

Jolly's age in 2 years $= 3x + 8 - 4 = 3x + 4$

Son's age in 2 years $= x + 6 - 4 = x + 2$

Total in 2 years $= 54 - 4 - 4 = 46$

Thus, we have the equation $x + 2 + 3x + 4 = 46$

OR $4x + 6 = 46$

EXAMPLE 3..

The price of two soccer balls and three hockey sticks is $173 while the price of five soccer balls and four hockey sticks is $338. Write two equations showing the cost of these items.

EXPLANATION

Let the price of soccer ball and hockey stick be b and h respectively

Then the total cost of two soccer balls and three hockey sticks will be $2b + 3h = 173$

Total cost of five soccer balls and four hockey sticks will be $5b + 4h = 338$

The two required equations are $2b + 3h = 173$ and $5b + 4h = 338$

ONE-VARIABLE QUADRATIC EQUATIONS

Sometimes, we may meet problems in life whose solutions can be arrived at by forming quadratic equations. The solution of these problems is then transformed to solutions of quadratic equations. In this section, we will look at how we can form quadratic equations from a given context.

EXAMPLE 1 ....

A two-digit number is such that the product of its digits is 24. When the position of the figures is interchanged, the new figure becomes 36 less than the original digit. Write a quadratic equation that would determine the value of the digits.

EXPLANATION

Let the digits be a and b where a is in the tens position and b in the ones position.

Then the number is ab

The product is $ab = 24$

The value of the number is $10a + b$ since that of a is $10a$ (in tens position) and $b \times 1 = b$ (in once position).

The value of the original number is $10a + b$

When the values are interchanged, the new number is ba whose value is $10a + b$

The difference is $10a + b - (10b + a) = 36$

$$9a - 9b = 36$$

Or

$$a - b = 4$$

Since $ab = 24$; hence
$$a = \frac{24}{b}$$

We then substitute into the above equation to get $\quad \dfrac{24}{b} - b = 4$

Multiplying through by b, we get $\quad 24 - b^2 = 4b$

Thus, the required equation is $\quad b^2 + 4b - 24 = 0$

EXAMPLE 2 ....

A piece of land is in form of a rectangle. The product of the length and the width is 510 square yards. If the distance around the piece of land is 98 yards, write one equation that would lead to the determination of one of the sides of the rectangle.

EXPLANATION

Let the length and the width be *l* be *w*

Thus the product of the length and the width is $lw = 510$ or $l = \dfrac{510}{w}$

The distance round the piece of land is the perimeter $= 2(l + w) = 98$

We now substitute for *l* to get

$$2\left(\frac{510}{w} + w\right) = 98$$

$$\left(\frac{510}{w} + w\right) = 49$$

Multiplying through by *w*, we get $510 + w^2 = 49w$

Thus, the required equation is $w^2 - 49w + 510 = 0$

LINEAR EXPRESSIONS WITH RATIONAL COEFFICIENTS

Linear expressions with rational coefficients are symbolic representations of quantifiable mathematical statements whose coefficients are fractions. In this section, we will deal with expressions that are linear, that is, have one variable. They include $\frac{x}{2} + \frac{1}{5}$, $\frac{5}{7} - \frac{5}{3}x$ and $\frac{4}{9}x$ among others.

To add or subtract these expressions we do so to the like's terms and use the least common multiple to of denominator to help reduce the complexity of the expression.

Multiplication implies multiplying numerators and denominators separately together with cancellation using common factor.

To divide them, we multiply by the reciprocal of the dividend the multiply.

EXAMPLE 1 ....

Simplify

$$\left(\frac{4}{5}x + \frac{1}{3}\right) - \left(\frac{5}{6} - \frac{3}{10}x\right)$$

EXPLANATION

$$\left(\frac{4}{5}x + \frac{1}{3}\right) - \left(\frac{5}{6} - \frac{3}{10}x\right) = \frac{4}{5}x + \frac{1}{3} - \frac{5}{6} + \frac{3}{10}x$$

We then collect like terms and add or subtract appropriately

$$\frac{4}{5}x + \frac{1}{3} - \frac{5}{6} + \frac{3}{10}x = \frac{1}{3} - \frac{5}{6} + \frac{4}{5}x + \frac{3}{10}x$$

$$= \frac{2-5}{6} + \frac{8+3}{10}x$$

$$= -\frac{3}{6} + \frac{11}{10}x$$

$$= \frac{11}{10}x - \frac{3}{6}$$

$$= \frac{11}{10}x - \frac{1}{2}$$

EXAMPLE 2 ....

Multiply $\frac{23}{7}x - \frac{2}{3}$ by $\frac{4}{9}x - \frac{3}{16}$

EXPLANATION

$$\left(\frac{23}{7}x - \frac{2}{3}\right)\left(\frac{4}{9}x - \frac{3}{16}\right) = \left(\frac{23}{7}x \times \frac{4}{9}x\right) - \left(\frac{23}{7}x \times \frac{3}{16}\right) - \left(\frac{2}{3} \times \frac{4}{9}x\right) + \left(\frac{2}{3} \times \frac{3}{16}\right)$$

$$= \frac{92}{63}x^2 - \frac{69}{112}x - \frac{8}{27}x + \frac{1}{8}$$

$$= \frac{92}{63}x^2 - \frac{1863+896}{3024}x + \frac{1}{8}$$

$$= \frac{92}{63}x^2 - \frac{2759}{3024}x + \frac{1}{8}$$

EXAMPLE 3

$$\text{Divide } \frac{5}{18}x - \frac{10}{21} \text{ by } \frac{x}{3}.$$

EXPLANATION

We have

$$\left(\frac{5}{18}x - \frac{10}{21}\right) \div \frac{x}{3} = \left(\frac{5}{18}x - \frac{10}{21}\right) \times \frac{3}{x}$$

$$= \frac{15x}{18x} - \frac{30}{21x}$$

$$= \frac{5}{6} - \frac{10}{7x}$$

LINEAR EXPRESSIONS AND WORD-TO-SYMBOL TRANSLATIONS

A times, there are problems that requires one to come up with symbolic representations of expressions from text. This is facilitated by the identification of keywords that imply the operation to use and the quantity used. In this section, we will write expressions from the given text.

EXAMPLE 1

Alice is 5.3 inches taller than Paul. Write an expression showing their total height.

EXPLANATION

Let Paul's height be h

Alice's height will be $5.3 + h$

Total height is $h + 5.3 + h = 5.3 + 2h$

EXAMPLE 2

Pipe A takes t hours to fill a tank while pipe B takes 2 fewer hours to fill the same tank. If pipe C takes two times faster than pipe B, write an expression showing the sum of hours taken to fill the tanks if they are allowed to run at different times.

EXPLANATION

Time taken by pipe $A = t$ hours

Time taken by pipe $B = t - 2$

Time taken by pipe C = half that of

$$B = \frac{t-2}{2}$$

$$\text{Total time} = t + t - 2 + \frac{t-2}{2} = 2t - 2 + \frac{t}{2} - 1$$

We collect the like terms

$$= 2t + \frac{1}{2}t - 1 - 2$$

$$= 2\frac{1}{2}t - 1 - 2$$

$$= 2\frac{1}{2}t - 3$$

$$= \frac{5}{2}t - 3$$

EXAMPLE 3..

Janine's has 2 pieces of candies more than half of what James has. Peter has four more pieces of candies than James. Taking Janine's number of candies as c, write an expression showing the sum of pieces of candies the three have altogether.

EXPLANATION

Let James have x pieces of candies

Janine will have

$$2 + \frac{1}{2}x$$

Peter has $x + 4$

We as asked to use c as our unknown. Since c is the number of candies Janine has, we have

$$2 + \frac{1}{2}x = c$$

We express x in terms of c

$$2 + \frac{1}{2}x = c \text{ implies } \frac{1}{2}x = c - 2 \text{ hence } x = 2(c - 2) = 2c - 4$$

Thus, James has $x = 2c - 4$ piece of candies

Janine has c pieces of candies

Peter has $x + 4 = 2c - 4 + 4 = 2c$ pieces of candies

The sum will be $2c - 4 + c + 2c = 5c - 4$

POLYNOMIALS

A polynomial is an expression having one or more algebraic terms with positive integer powers on the variables. Example, $2 + 3x$, $1 - x^2 + 5x^3$, $x^4 - 3x^2 + 3$ and so on. In this section, we will only consider polynomials with two terms only.

Addition and subtraction implies adding and subtracting terms with like terms only (terms whose variables are raised to the same power) Wile multiplication implies multiply a terms by any term in the other expression. This is best done by used of brackets.

Division is done by factorization.

EXAMPLE 1 ....

Add $3a - 56$ to $41 - 7a$

EXPLANATION

$$3a - 56 + 41 - 7a = 3a - 7a + 41 - 56$$

Upon collecting the like terms together

$$= -4a - 15$$

EXAMPLE 2 ....

Subtract $2x - 12x^3$ from $4x^2 + 14x^3$

EXPLANATION

$$4x^2 + 14x^3 - (2x - 12x^3) = 4x^2 + 14x^3 - 2x + 12x^3$$

(Upon opening the brackets)

$$= 4x^2 - 2x + 14x^3 + 12x^3$$
$$= 4x^2 - 2x + 28x^3$$

EXAMPLE 3 ....

Find the product of the following expressions $5 - 2x$ and $12x^2 - 4$

EXPLANATION

$$(12x^2 - 4)(5 - 2x) = 12x^2(5 - 2x) - 4(5 - 2x)$$
$$= 60x^2 - 24x^3 - 20 + 8x$$
$$= -24x^3 + 60x^2 + 8x - 20$$

EXAMPLE 4..

Divide $9x^3 - 36x^2$ by $12x - 3x^2$

EXPLANATION

We factorize each expression

$$9x^3 - 36x^2 = 9x^2(x - 4)$$
$$12x - 3x^2 = -3x(-4 + x)$$
$$= \frac{9x^2(x - 4)}{-3x(x - 4)}$$
$$= -3x \qquad \text{(Upon cancellation)}$$

POLYNOMIAL EXPRESSIONS AND WORD-TO-SYMBOL TRANSLATIONS

Just like other expression that we have already dealt with, life some life problems can be solved by expressing them in terms of polynomials then determining their solution mathematically. In this section, we will try to come up with polynomials given the word problem.

EXAMPLE 1 ....

James would like to make a rectangular based flour garden whose distance around the garden is 14 feet. If the length of the garden is six times the width, form a polynomial equation that would be used to determine the width of the garden.

EXPLANATION

Let the width be w

The length would be $6w$

$$\text{Perimeter} = 2(l + w) = 14$$

Upon substitution, we get

$$2(6w + w) = 14$$
$$7w = 7$$

Thus the required polynomial equation is $7w - 7 = 0$

EXAMPLE 2..

Determine the expression showing product of three consecutive even numbers.

EXPLANATION

Since an even number must be divisible by 2, we take any number say x and multiply it by 2 so that it represents the least even numbers.

The least numbers is $2x$

The difference between the least and the next even number is, hence, the next number is $2x + 2$

The third even number will be $2x + 2 + 2 = 2x + 4$

The product of these three is $(2x)(2x + 2)(2x + 4)$

$$(2x)(2x + 2)(2x + 4) = (4x^2 + 4x)(2x + 4)$$
$$= 4x^2(2x + 4) + 4x(2x + 4)$$
$$= 8x^3 + 16x^2 + 4x^2 + 16x = 8x^3 + 20x^2 + 16x$$

The required expression is $8x^3 + 20x^2 + 16x$

EXAMPLE 3..

The length of a rectangle is 4 units less than three times the width. If the area of the rectangle is 96 sq. in, write a polynomial equation that would be used to determine the width of the rectangle.

EXPLANATION

Let the width be $w = x$

Three times the width is $3x$

The length will be $l = 3x - 4$

The area $= lw = 96$ or $lw - 96 = 0$

Upon substitution, we have

$$x(3x - 4) - 90 = 0$$

$$3x^2 - 4x - 90 = 0$$

Thus, the required equation is

$$3x^2 - 4x - 90 = 0$$

RATIONAL EXPRESSIONS

Rational fractions are expressions in form of a fraction where the numerator and the denominator are polynomials. Example

$$\frac{3}{x}, \frac{2x+1}{5x^2+6x-1}, \frac{1}{x-1}$$

among others

Addition and subtraction of these rational fractions is done using the concept of least common multiple just like fractions are added and subtracted. The like terms are then added and subtracted accordingly.

Multiplication is done by multiplying the numerators as well as the denominators. Cancellation is then done when there is a common factor.

Division is done when the divisor is multiplied by it's reciprocal.

EXAMPLE 1 ....

Simplify to single fraction

$$\frac{2}{x} + \frac{3}{4x}$$

EXPLANATION

The least common multiple of the denominator is $4x$

$$\frac{2}{x} + \frac{3}{4x} = \frac{2(4)+3}{4x}$$

$$= \frac{11}{4x}$$

EXAMPLE 2...

Subtract $\dfrac{2x}{x+1}$ from $\dfrac{1}{x^2-1}$

EXPLANATION

$$\frac{1}{x^2-1}-\frac{2x}{x+1}$$
$$x^2-1=x^2-1^2=(x-1)(x+1)$$
$$=-24$$

But $x^2 - 1 = x^2 - 1^2 = (x - 1)(x + 1)$ from application the application of the quadratic identity $a^2 - b^2 = (a + b)(a - b)$

$$\frac{1}{x^2-1}-\frac{2x}{x+1}=\frac{1}{(x-1)(x+1)}-\frac{2x}{x+1}$$

The least common multiple of $(x - 1)(x + 1)$ and $x + 1$ is $(x - 1)(x + 1)$

$$\frac{1}{(x-1)(x+1)}-\frac{2x}{x+1}=\frac{1-2x(x-1)}{(x-1)(x+1)}$$

$$=\frac{1-2x^2+2x}{(x-1)(x+1)}$$

EXAMPLE 3...

Simplify

$$\frac{6x}{3-x}\times\frac{4x-12}{x}$$

EXPLANATION

We factorize and multiply the numerators and the denominators separately ten carry out cancellation

$$\frac{1}{x^2-1}-\frac{2x}{x+1}$$
$$x^2-1=x^2-1^2=(x-1)(x+1)$$
$$=-24$$

EXAMPLE 4..

Simplify

$$\frac{4x+4}{3x} \div \frac{x^2+2x+1}{15x^2}$$

EXPLANATION

Division implies multiplication by the reciprocal of the divisor

$$\frac{4x+4}{3x} \div \frac{x^2+2x+1}{15x^2} = \frac{4x+4}{3x} \times \frac{15x^2}{x^2+2x+1}$$

But $x^2+2x+1 = x^2+x+x+1 = x(x+1)+1(x+1) = (x+1)(x+1) = (x+1)^2$

$$4x+4 = 4(x+1)$$

$$= \frac{4(x+1)}{3x} \times \frac{15x^2}{(x+1)^2} = \frac{4(15x^2)(x+1)}{3x(x+1)^2}$$

$$= \frac{4(15x^2)}{3x(x+1)}$$

$$= \frac{20x}{(x+1)}$$

RATIONAL EXPRESSIONS AND WORD-TO-SYMBOL TRANSLATIONS

We also encounter word problems that can be solved by transforming them into rational fractions after which they are solved. Let us consider a number of the examples.

EXAMPLE 1 ....

A tractor takes r hours while another takes 3r hours to plow 7 acres of land. If the begin together at the same time, find the fraction of the work that remains after one hour.

EXPLANATION

In one hour, the first tractor completes $\frac{1}{r}$ hours of the work

In the same time, tractor 2 takes $\frac{1}{3r}$

The fraction of work done after one hour =

$$\frac{1}{r} + \frac{1}{3r} = \frac{3+1}{3r} = \frac{4}{3r}$$

The remaining fraction of work is

$$1 - \frac{4}{3r} = \frac{3r-4}{3r}$$

EXAMPLE 2...

The area of a triangle is given in terms of a variable x as $2x^2 + 2x + 6$. If one is the base is $x + 2$ determine its base.

We first factorize the quadratic equation

$$2x^2 + 7x + 6 = 2x^2 + 4x + 3x + 6$$
$$= 2x(x+2) + 3(x+2)$$
$$= (2x+3)(x+2)$$
$$\text{Area} = \frac{1}{2}bh = (2x+3)(x+2)$$

Upon substitution, we have

$$\frac{(x+2)h}{2} = (2x+3)(x+2)$$

Dividing through by $(x + 2)$, we get

$$\frac{h}{2} = 2x + 3$$

Thus $h = 4x + 6$

SOLVING SYSTEM OF TWO SIMULTANEOUS LINEAR EQUATIONS

A system of simultaneous linear equations refers to a pair or more collections of linear equations that may have common solutions. In this section, we will only consider systems having two linear equations. These equations can be solved by a number of methods such as elimination, substitution, matrices or graphical methods, however, in this section, we will only use the first two.

EXAMPLE 1 .....

Use substitution method to find the value of x and y is $x + y = 9$ and $x - y = 3$

EXPLANATION

From $x - y = 3$, we have $x = 3 + y$

We now substitute this into the other equation to get $3 + y + y = 9$

Thus $3 + 2y = 9$; $2y = 6$; $y = 3$

But $x = 3 + y = 3 + 3 = 6$

Thus $x = 6$, $y = 3$

EXAMPLE 2 .....

Solve the following simultaneous equation

$$3x - 2y = 3; \quad 2x + 4y = 34$$

EXPLANATION

We multiply the first equation by 2 then add to the other equation

$$6x - 4y = 6; 2x + 4y = 34$$

Adding the two, we get $8x = 40$; $x = 5$

From the first equation, we substitute for y to get x, thus

$$15 - 2y = 3; \quad 2y = 12; \quad y = 6$$

Thus $x = 5$, $y = 6$

EXAMPLE 3

Solve the following simultaneous equation

$$5y - 2x = 26; 3y - 4x = 24$$

EXPLANATION

We multiply the first equation by 2 then add to the other equation

$$10y - 4x = 52; \quad 3y - 4x = 24$$

Subtracting the second from the first equation, we get

$$7y = 28; \quad y = 4$$

From the second equation, we have

$$12 - 4x = 24; \quad 4x = -12; \quad x = -3$$

Thus $x = -3$ and $y = 4$

WRAPPING IT UP

In this section we have looked at various algebraic manipulations. We began by looking at representations of algebraic functions and proceeded to formation of expressions and equations from word statements. This involved, linear, quadratic, polynomials and rational functions and functions we rational coefficients. We have also looked at addition, subtraction, multiplication and division of these expressions. We have finalized by looking at simultaneous expressions.

SIMPLIFICATION OF SIMPLE ALGEBRAIC AND NUMERIC FORMS

What You Need to Know About This Section?

Most problems we encounter involves numerical values, simple algebraic equations and expressions. Therefore, it is necessary that we understand how to handle these two concepts. Our main aim will be solutions of linear and quadratic equations and evaluation of polynomials and rational expression. We will then look at operations of fractions and the preliminary concepts required to discuss these operations.

MATH TOPICS

- Solve quadratic equations in one variable with rational coefficients and real solutions, using appropriate methods (i.e. quadratic formula, completing the square, factoring, inspection) (Reference 1.41).
- Evaluate linear expressions by substituting integers for unknown quantities (Reference 1.42).
- Evaluate polynomial expressions by substituting integers for unknown quantities (Reference 1.43).
- Evaluate rational expressions by substituting integers for unknown quantities (Reference 1.44).
- Evaluate linear and quadratic functions for values in their domain when represented using function notation (Reference 1.45).
- Solve one-variable linear equations with rational number coefficients, including equations whose solutions require expanding expressions using the distributive property and collecting like terms or equations with coefficients represented by letters (Reference 1.46).
- Order fractions and decimals, including on a number line (Reference 1.47).
- Apply number properties involving multiples and factors, such as using the least common multiple, greatest common factor, or distributive property to rewrite numeric expression (Reference 1.48).

✐ Apply rules of exponents in numerical expressions with rational exponents to write equivalent expressions with rational exponents (Reference 1.49).

✐ Perform addition, subtraction, multiplication, and division on rational numbers (Reference 1.50).

INTRODUCTION

In this section, we are going to look at simplification of algebraic forms, mainly expressions and fractions. The expressions to be considered will be rational expressions and polynomials with single variables. The equations will only be quadratic and linear. One of the main aim would be evaluating these expressions and applying the distributive property that is very common in simplification of algebraic forms. We will also look at some simplifications of numerical forms mainly operation of fractions and representation of numerical expressions with rational exponents. This will in fact be possible having discussed ordering of decimals and fractions, discussions of factors and multiples and their applications.

SOLVING QUADRATIC EQUATIONS

A quadratic equation is an equation whose highest powers, degree, is 2. It is generally given in the form $ax^2 + bx + c = 0$ where a cannot be zero, a, b and c are real numbers. For our case, we consider the case where a, b and c are rational numbers. Example, $2x^2 - 3 = 0$, $x^2 + \frac{1}{4}x - \frac{1}{2} = 0$ among others. Since the highest power is 2, they have two solutions. These solutions may be equal or not equal. They may be real or imaginary. In our situation, we will be concerned with equations whose solutions are real.

Solution of these equations is determined by inspection, factorization and quadratic formula among others.

The quadratic formula based on the general quadratic equation above is given by

$$x = \frac{-b \pm \sqrt{b^2 - 4ac}}{2a}$$

EXAMPLE 1 ....

Find the solution of $x^2 - 16 = 0$

EXPLANATION

$x^2 - 16 = 0$ is equivalent to $x^2 = 16$

This can be solved by inspection. What number can we square to get 16, the number is 4 and -4.

Verification,

$$4^2 = (-4)^2 = 16$$

Thus

$$x = -4, \ x = 4$$

EXAMPLE 2 ....

Find the solution of $2x^2 - x - 15$ by factorization methods.

EXPLANATION

To expand the middle term, x, we multiply the 2 by -15 to get -30. Two factors of -30 that will add up to -1 is -6 and 5. Thus, we have

$$2x^2 - x - 15 = 2x^2 - 6x + 5x - 15 = 0$$
$$= (2x + 5)(x - 3) = 0$$
$$= 2x(x - 3) + 5(x - 3) = 0$$

Thus, we have

$$2x + 5 = 0, \ x - 3 = 0$$

Thus, we have

$$x = -\frac{5}{2}, \ x = 3$$

EXAMPLE 3..

Use completing square method and the quadratic formula to determine the solution of $4x^2 - 4x - 3$.

EXPLANATION

$$4x^2 - 4x - 3 = \left(4x^2 - 4x\right) - 3 = 0$$

$$= 4\left(x^2 - x\right) - 3 = 0$$

$$= 4\left(x^2 - x + \left(\frac{1}{2}\right)^2 - \left(\frac{1}{2}\right)^2\right) - 3 = 0$$

$$= 4\left(x^2 - x + \left(\frac{1}{2}\right)^2\right) - 4 = 0$$

$$= 4\left(x^2 - x + \left(\frac{1}{2}\right)^2\right) - 1 - 3 = 0$$

$$= 4\left(x^2 - x + \left(\frac{1}{2}\right)^2 - \frac{1}{4}\right) - 3 = 0$$

Using the quadratic identity for perfect square $(a + b)^2 = a^2 + 2ab + b^2$, we have

$$= 4\left(x - \frac{1}{2}\right)^2 - 4 = 0$$

$$= 4\left(x - \frac{1}{2}\right)^2 = 4$$

$$= \left(x - \frac{1}{2}\right)^2 = 1$$

Taking square roots on both sides, we have

$$= x - \frac{1}{2} = \pm 1$$

$$x = \pm 1 + \frac{1}{2}$$

$$x = \pm 1 + \frac{1}{2}$$

Thus,

$$x = 1 + \frac{1}{2} = \frac{3}{2}$$

$$x = -1 + \frac{1}{2} = -\frac{1}{2}$$

Thus

$$x = \frac{3}{2} \quad \text{or} \quad x = \frac{1}{2}$$

By quadratic formula, we have

$$x = \frac{-b \pm \sqrt{b^2 - 4ac}}{2a}$$

From the example, we have $a = 4$, $b = -4$, $c = -3$

Upon substitution, we have

$$x = \frac{4 - 8}{8} = -\frac{4}{8} = -\frac{1}{2}$$

$$x = \frac{4 - 8}{8} = -\frac{4}{8} = -\frac{1}{2}$$

$$x = \frac{4 + 8}{8} = \frac{12}{8} = \frac{3}{2}$$

LINEAR EXPRESSIONS

Linear expressions are algebraic expressions where the highest power of the independent variable, the x variable, is 1. For example, $2x + 3$, $3 - 2(4x - 2)$ among others. The aim of this section is to determine the value of the expression at the stated points. This is done by substitution.

EXAMPLE 1 ....

Given that $x = 2$, find the value of $5 + 2(7x - 3)$

EXPLANATION

We carry out substitution,

$$5 + 2(7(2) - 3) = 5 + 2(14 - 3)$$
$$= 5 + 2(11)$$
$$= 5 + 22 = 27[$$

EXAMPLE 2 ....

Given that $t = -6$, evaluate $11 - 4t$

EXPLANATION

We substitute for t to get $11 - 4(-6) = 11 + 24 = 35$

POLYNOMIAL EXPRESSIONS

Polynomials are expressions with variables having integer powers. Example, $x^2 + 2x - 5$, $x^6 - 65x^3 - 2x - 3$, $x^4 - 64x - 2$ among others. Our interest is to determine the value of these polynomials a certain values of the variable x.

EXAMPLE 1 ....

Given that $r = -1$, find the value of $4r^2 + 7r - 9$.

EXPLANATION

We carry out substitution,

$$4(-1)^2 + 7(-1) - 9 = 4 - 7 - 9$$
$$= -12$$

EXAMPLE 2 ....

Find the difference between the values of the polynomials at $6x^3 - 5x^2 + 8x + 2$ at $x = -2$ and $x = 3$.

iGlobal GED Math Study Guide

EXPLANATION

At $x = -2$, we have

$$6(-2)^3 - 5(-2)^2 + 8(-2) + 2 = 6(-8) - 5(4) + 8(-2) + 2$$
$$= -48 - 20 - 16 + 2$$
$$= -82$$

At $x = 3$, we have

$$6(3)^3 - 5(3)^2 + 8(3) + 2 = 6(27) - 5(9) + 8(3) + 2$$
$$= 162 - 45 + 24 + 2$$
$$= 143$$

The difference between the two values is $143 - -82 = 225$

RATIONAL EXPRESSIONS

Rational expressions are expressions in form of a fraction where the numerator and the denominator is a polynomial. In this section, we are interested in evaluating the values of these expressions at given points.

EXAMPLE 1 ....

Find the value of the following expressions at the $x = -4$.

$$\frac{x^2 - 4x}{6x^2 + 8}$$

EXPLANATION

We substitute for the value of x

$$\frac{x^2 - 4x}{6x^2 + 8} = \frac{(-4)^2 - 4(-4)}{6(-4)^2 + 8}$$
$$= \frac{16 + 16}{6(16) + 18}$$
$$= \frac{32}{114}$$
$$= \frac{16}{57}$$

EXAMPLE 2...

Evaluate the expression

$$\frac{9x^2 + 7}{4x - 3}$$

at $x = -6$

EXPLANATION

We carry out substitution for x, thus

$$\frac{9x^2 + 7}{4x - 3} = \frac{9(-6)^2 + 7}{4(-6) - 3}$$

$$= \frac{324 + 7}{-24 - 3}$$

$$= \frac{331}{-27}$$

EXAMPLE 3...

Find the value of

$$\frac{2 - x}{x^2 + 6x - 7} \quad \text{if } x = -4$$

EXPLANATION

We carry out substitution

$$\frac{2 - x}{x^2 + 6x - 7} = \frac{2 - (-4)}{(-4)^2 + 6(-4) - 7}$$

$$= \frac{6}{16 - 24 - 7}$$

$$= \frac{6}{-15}$$

$$= -\frac{2}{5}$$

LINEAR AND QUADRATIC FUNCTIONS

A linear function is an equation where a variable, the dependent variable (say y), is expressed in terms in terms of another, independent variable (say x), with the former having the highest power of 1. Example $y = ax + b$ where a and b are real numbers and a cannot be zero. The functional representation of linear function is $f(x) = ax + b$ where $y = f(x)$ is termed to be a function of x, that is, it is basically expressed in terms of x.

A quadratic function is an equation where the highest power of the independent variable being 2.

We may generally represent it as $y = ax^2 + bx + c$ where a, b and c are real numbers and c cannot be zero. In terms of its functional relationships, we write $f(x) = ax^2 + bx + c$. All values of x that can be substituted into the function, either linear or quadratic to give use a number (a value) on evaluation, are said to belong to a collection of values called the domain. These values are called inputs while the resultant values after evaluation are called outputs values. In this section, we will evaluate the functions at values in their domains.

EXAMPLE 1 ....

Find the output of the function $f(x) = 3x - 1$ if the input is 2.

EXPLANATION

Since 2 is the input, we have $x = 2$

Therefore, the output will be $f(2) = 3(2) - 1 = 6 - 1 = 5$

EXAMPLE 2..........

Evaluate each of the following functions at $x = -1$ and $x = 9$.

(i). $g(x) = 4x^2 - 2x + 1$

(ii). $h(x) = 4 - 6x$

EXPLANATION

(i). At $x = -1$, we have

$$g(-1) = 4(-1)^2 - 2(-1) + 1$$
$$= 4(1) + 2 + 1 = 7$$

At $x = 9$, we have

$$g(9) = 4(9)^2 - 2(9) + 1$$
$$= 4(81) - 2(9) + 1$$
$$= 324 - 18 + 1 = 307$$

(ii). At $x = -1$, we have

$$h(-1) = 4 - 6(-1)$$
$$= 4 + 6 = 10$$

At $x = 9$, we have

$$h(9) = 4 - 6(9)$$
$$= -50$$

SOLVING ONE-VARIABLE LINEAR EQUATIONS

One variable linear equations are equations whose highest power on the independent variable is one. They are generally given as $y = ax + b$ where a and b are constant and a not being equal zero, however, sometimes we meet them in other equivalent forms for instance $y = 3 - 3(x + 1)$.

In this section we are concerned with solving such forms of linear equations whose coefficients are rational numbers.

EXAMPLE 1 ....

Find the value of x if $\frac{1}{2} - \frac{1}{3}(x-3) = 0$

EXPLANATION

$$\frac{1}{2} - \frac{1}{3}(x-3) = 0$$

We first simplify the problem in the brackets, that is, multiply $-\frac{1}{3}$ by everything in the brackets (a process called distributive property)

$$\frac{1}{2} - \frac{1}{3}x + 1 = 0$$

On collecting like terms on one side, we have

$$-\frac{1}{3}x = -1 - \frac{1}{2}$$

Using the property of equivalent fractions, 1 has two halfs hence

$$1 = 2\left(\frac{1}{2}\right) = \frac{2}{2}$$

Substituting above, we have

$$-\frac{1}{3}x = -\frac{2}{2} - \frac{1}{2} = -\frac{3}{2}$$

Thus

$$-\frac{1}{3}x = -\frac{3}{2}$$

Multiplying through by −3, we get

$$x = -\frac{3}{2} \times -3 = \frac{9}{2} = 4\frac{1}{2}.$$

$$x = 4\frac{1}{2}$$

EXAMPLE 2..

Solve the equation

$$2\left(\frac{3}{4}x - 5\right) + \frac{2}{5} = 4\left(\frac{1}{4}x + \frac{1}{5}\right)$$

EXPLANATION

We first simplify the problem in the brackets, that is, multiply what is outside the bracket with everything in the brackets (a process called distributive property)

$$\left(2 \times \frac{3}{4}x\right) - \left(2 \times 5\right) + \frac{2}{5} = \left(4 \times \frac{1}{4}x\right) + \left(4 \times \frac{1}{5}\right)$$

Upon multiplication, we get

$$\frac{3}{2}x - 10 + \frac{2}{5} = x + \frac{4}{5}$$

Collecting like terms on either sides, we have

$$\frac{3}{2}x - x = \frac{4}{5} - \frac{2}{5} + 10$$

If we express x to have the same denominator as $\frac{3}{2}x$, we have $x = \frac{2}{2}x$.

Likewise, letting 10 has a denominator of 5, we have $\frac{50}{5}$

Thus, we have

$$\frac{3}{2}x - \frac{2}{2}x = \frac{4}{5} - \frac{2}{5} + \frac{50}{5}$$

Subtracting and adding respectively, we have

$$\frac{1}{2}x = \frac{52}{5}$$

Multiplying through by 2, we get

$$x = \frac{52}{5} \times 2 = \frac{104}{5}$$

$$x = \frac{104}{5} = 20\frac{4}{5}$$

iGlobal GED Math Study Guide

ORDER FRACTIONS AND DECIMALS

In most cases, we come across situation where we are required to compare numbers, especially decimals, fractions or a mixture. The best approach is usually to multiply the numbers by 100% then compare the results. The comparison may lead to ordering numbers in ascending or descending order. Ascending orders implies arranging numbers from the lowest to the highest while descending order implies writing numbers from the highest. In this section, we will order numbers and also plot them on the number line.

EXAMPLE 1

Order the following numbers in ascending order.

(i). 0.3, 0.54, 0.60, 0.009

(ii). $\dfrac{4}{5}, \dfrac{2}{3}, \dfrac{3}{4}, \dfrac{1}{2}, \dfrac{5}{6}$

(iii). 0.52, $\dfrac{1}{2}$, 0.7, $\dfrac{2}{3}$

EXPLANATION

We multiply the numbers by 100% and compare the numbers by looking at the largest number in a given place value, from the left to the right.

(i). 0.3, 0.54, 0.60, 0.009

Multiplying by 100%, we get 30%, 54%, 60%, 0.9%

From the list, the smallest percentage is 0.9%, 30%, 54% then 60%

Thus, when arranged in ascending order, we will have 0.9%, 30%, 54%, 60%

(ii). $\dfrac{4}{5}, \dfrac{2}{3}, \dfrac{3}{4}, \dfrac{1}{2}, \dfrac{5}{6}$

Multiplying by 100%, we have

$$\dfrac{4}{5} \times 100\% = 80\%, \quad \dfrac{2}{3} \times 100\% = 66.67\%, \quad \dfrac{3}{4} \times 100\% = 75\%$$

$$\dfrac{1}{2} \times 100\% = 50\%, \quad \dfrac{5}{6} \times 100\% = 83.33\%$$

The smallest percentage is 50%, then 66.67%, 75%, 80% then the largest one is 83.33%

Comparing with the original numbers, we get the required list

$$\frac{1}{2}, \frac{2}{3}, \frac{3}{4}, \frac{4}{5}, \frac{5}{6}$$

(iii). $0.52, \frac{1}{2}, 0.7, \frac{2}{3}$

Multiply the numbers by 100%, we get 52%, 50%, 70% and 66.67%

Hence, the smallest number is 50%, 52%, 66.67%, 70%

The required list is $\frac{1}{2}, 0.52, \frac{2}{3}, 0.7$

EXAMPLE 2..

Estimate the location of the following numbers on the number line

$$\frac{13}{5}, 0.2, \frac{1}{3}, \frac{7}{4}, 3.6,$$

We express the numbers in decimal form

$$\frac{13}{5} = 2\frac{3}{5} = 2.6, \frac{1}{3} = 0.3333, \frac{7}{4} = 1\frac{3}{4} = 1.75$$

Thus, we have the numbers as 26, 0.2, 0.3333, 1.75 and 3.6

In ascending order, we will have 0.2, 0.3333, 1.75, 2.6, 3.6

0.2 and 0.3333 are less than 0.5 but more than 0, hence they are in between 0.5.

1.75 is more than 1 and less than 2. In fact it is more than 1.5 by 0.25 (half of 0.5). This means that it is between 1.5 and 2.

2.6 is more than 2 and less than 3 hence it is between the two numbers. Furthermore, it is more than 2.5 by 0.1 hence it is slightly more than 2.5.

3.6 is more than 3 and less than 4 hence it is between the two numbers. Furthermore, it is more than 3.5 by 0.1 hence it is slightly more than 3.5.

Upon plotting, we have

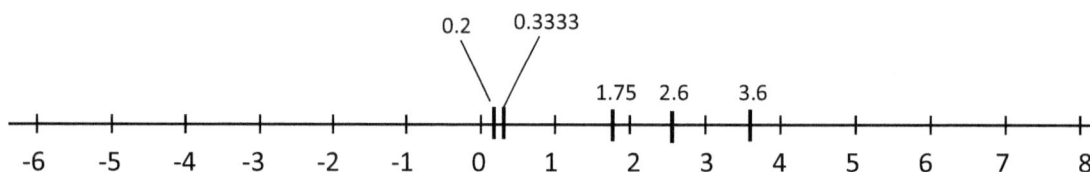

LEAST COMMON MULTIPLE (LCM), GREATEST COMMON FACTOR (GCF), AND DISTRIBUTIVE PROPERTY

Factors are numbers that divides other numbers while multiples are number that are as a result of the product of a number with integers. Factors may be prime numbers or not. Prime numbers are numbers that can be divided by one and themselves. When factors are prime numbers, we call them prime factors. Considering two or more numbers we may get the prime factors that are common to both or all these numbers. When we least all these prime factors, we multiply them to get the highest or the greatest common factor (GCF).

Likewise, given a group of numbers, we may list their multiple then select the smallest multiple from the list of all multiples.

We will also express the sum of difference of numbers as a product of a factor and a difference of other factors.

EXAMPLE 1 ....

Find the Least Common Multiple (L.C.M) of 6, 15 and 9.

EXPLANATION

We use factorization method, divide the numbers by prime factors until the number reduces to 1. When the number cannot be divided by a given prime factor, we carry it forward.

2	6	9	15
3	3	9	15
3	1	3	5
5	1	1	5
	1	1	1

The L.C.M is $2 \times 3 \times 3 \times 5 = 90$

EXAMPLE 2

Find the Greatest Common Factor (G.C.D) of 24, 36 and 54.

EXPLANATION

We divide all the numbers at the same time a prime factor that must divide all the numbers completely without a remainder.

2	24	36	54
3	12	18	27
	4	6	9

We end at this point because we do not have a common factor

The G.C.D = 2 × 3 = 6

EXAMPLE 3

Express 36 − 27 as a product of a factor a difference of two numbers.

We find the common factor between the two, the common factor is 9.

$$36 = 9 \times 4 \text{ and } 27 = 9 \times 3$$

Hence
$$36 - 27 = (9 \times 4) - (9 \times 3)$$

Since 9 is common in the brackets, we take it outside so that we remain with

$$36 - 27 = 9(4 - 3)$$

RULES FOR EXPONENTS

A number is written in an exponential notation if it is in the form a^b where a is the base and b the exponent. Some of the rules relevant to this section are $\sqrt[n]{a} = a^{\frac{1}{n}}$ and $\left(\sqrt[n]{a}\right)^m = a^{\frac{m}{n}}$. In this section, we are going to express the numerical expressions with rational exponents into equivalent expressions with rational exponents

EXAMPLE 1 ....

Write $\sqrt[4]{8} - \sqrt[3]{27}$ in terms of the equivalent expression with rational exponents

EXPLANATION

Using $\sqrt[n]{a} = a^{\frac{1}{n}}$, we have $\sqrt[4]{8} = 8^{\frac{1}{4}}$ and $\sqrt[3]{27} = 27^{\frac{1}{3}}$

Thus, $\sqrt[4]{8} - \sqrt[3]{27} = 8^{\frac{1}{4}} - 27^{\frac{1}{3}}$

EXAMPLE 2 ....

Write the following expressions in terms of the equivalent expression with rational exponents

$$\sqrt[4]{6} + \left(\sqrt[6]{32}\right)^8$$

$$\left(\sqrt[4]{16}\right)^6 - \left(\sqrt[3]{36}\right)^6$$

EXPLANATION

Using $\sqrt[n]{a} = a^{\frac{1}{n}}$ and $\left(\sqrt[n]{a}\right)^m = a^{\frac{m}{n}}$, we have

$$\sqrt[4]{6} = 6^{\frac{1}{4}}, \ \left(\sqrt[6]{32}\right)^8 = 32^{\frac{6}{8}} = 32^{\frac{3}{4}}, \ \left(\sqrt[4]{16}\right)^6 = 16^{\frac{4}{6}} = 16^{\frac{2}{3}}, \ \left(\sqrt[3]{36}\right)^6 = 36^{\frac{3}{6}} = 36^{\frac{1}{3}}$$

Upon substitution, we have

(i). $\sqrt[4]{6} + \left(\sqrt[6]{32}\right)^8 = 6^{\frac{1}{4}} + 32^{\frac{3}{4}}$

(ii). $\left(\sqrt[4]{16}\right)^6 - \left(\sqrt[3]{36}\right)^6 = 16^{\frac{2}{3}} - 36^{\frac{1}{3}}$

ADDING, SUBTRACTING, MULTIPLYING, DIVIDING RATIONAL NUMBERS

Rational numbers are numbers written in the form $\frac{a}{b}$ where a and b are real numbers and b is not zero. Example $\frac{2}{5}, \frac{20}{3}, 2 = \frac{2}{1}, 0 = \frac{0}{3}$ and so on. To add and subtract rational numbers, we use the concept of equivalent fractions which well covered when we use the concept of Least Common Multiple. To multiply rational numbers, we multiply the numerators and the denominators separately and cancel out common factors. To divide rational numbers, we multiply the divisor by its reciprocal then follow the multiplication procedure.

EXAMPLE 1 ....

Simplify

(i). $\dfrac{2}{9} + \dfrac{4}{6}$

(ii). $2\dfrac{3}{4} - 1\dfrac{5}{7}$

EXPLANATION

(i). To add, we find the L.C.M of the denominators. The L.C.M of 9 and 6 is 18

We let 18 be the denominator of the new fraction

$$\frac{2}{9} + \frac{4}{6} = \frac{}{18}$$

Divide 18 by 9 and multiply the results by 2 to get 4. Write 4 in the numerator and to it add the results from the next fraction.

Divide 18 by 6 and multiply the results by 4 to get 12. Add 12 to 4

$$\frac{2}{9} + \frac{4}{6} = \frac{4+12}{18} = \frac{16}{18}$$

Simplifying the fraction as a simple fraction, we get $\dfrac{16}{18} = \dfrac{8}{9}$

Hence

$$\frac{2}{9} + \frac{4}{6} = \frac{8}{9}$$

(ii). Change the fractions to improper fractions

$$2\frac{3}{4} - 1\frac{5}{7} = \frac{11}{4} - \frac{12}{7}$$

iGlobal GED Math Study Guide

To subtract, we find the L.C.M of the denominators. The L.C.M of 4 and 7 is 28

We let 28 be the denominator of the new fraction

$$\frac{11}{4} - \frac{12}{7} = \frac{}{28}$$

Divide 28 by 4 and multiply the results by 11 to get 77. Write 77 in the numerator and to it subtract the results from the next fraction.

Divide 28 by 7 and multiply the results by 12 to get 48. Subtract 48 from 77

$$\frac{11}{4} - \frac{12}{7} = \frac{77-48}{28} = \frac{29}{28}$$

Simplifying the fraction as a simple fraction, we get $\frac{29}{28} = 1\frac{1}{28}$

$$2\frac{3}{4} - 1\frac{5}{7} = 1\frac{1}{28}$$

EXAMPLE 2..

Multiply

$$\frac{2}{3} \, by \, \frac{15}{14}$$

EXPLANATION

Multiplying $\frac{2}{3} \, by \, \frac{15}{14}$

We have

$$\frac{2}{3} \times \frac{15}{14} = \frac{2 \times 15}{3 \times 14}$$

Cancelling out common factors, we get

$$\frac{2 \times 15}{3 \times 14} = \frac{1 \times 5}{1 \times 7} = \frac{5}{7}$$

Thus, the results is $\frac{5}{7}$

EXAMPLE 3..

Simplify

$$\frac{12}{16} \sqrt{\frac{3}{8}}$$

EXPLANATION

By definition,

$$\frac{12}{16} \div \frac{3}{8} = \frac{12}{16} \times \frac{8}{3}$$

$$= \frac{12 \times 8}{16 \times 3}$$

Cancelling out the common factors, we get

$$= \frac{4 \times 1}{2 \times 1} = \frac{2}{1} = 2$$

WRAPPING IT UP

In this section, we have looked at solutions of equations; quadratic equations and evaluations of expressions such as linear, quadratic, polynomials, rational at given values of the independent variables. We have also introduced the functional notation of linear and quadratic equations and determined their output given the input. We have also looked at ordering and location of decimals and fractions on the numbers line. We have also looked at some rules of evaluating exponents with rational coefficients. Finally, we have looked at least common factors, greatest common factors and their application in addition, subtraction and division of rational numbers. Multiplication of such numbers was also looked at.

FORMS OF REPRESENTATION OF NUMERICAL NUMBERS AND THEIR APPLICATIONS

What You Need to Know About This Section?

Numerical numbers are not only expressed as we first knew them, as 1, 2, 3, 4, and so on, we also have different forms of representations. These representations are brought about due to different real life situations and problems that we meet. For instance, the area of a squares makes us think of a product of two equal numbers called a square, the determination of the side of a square makes us think of a number whose product is the area, a number called the square root. All these are representations of numbers in different forms. Other representations include, cubes, cube roots, scientific forms, percentages and ratios. In this session, we are going to discuss these representations together with their applications.

MATH TOPICS

✎ Perform computations and write numerical expressions with squares and square roots of rational numbers (Reference 1.51).

✎ Perform computations and write numerical expressions with cubes and cube roots of rational numbers (Reference 1.52).

✎ Solve one-step or multi-step arithmetic, real world problems involving the four operations with rational numbers, including those involving scientific notation (Reference 1.53).

✎ Solve multistep, arithmetic, real-world problems using ratios or proportions including those that require converting units of measure (Reference 1.54).

✎ Solve two-step, arithmetic, real world problems involving percents. Examples include but are not limited to: simple interest, tax, markups and markdowns, gratuities and commissions, percent increase and decrease (Reference 1.55).

INTRODUCTION

Determination of area of a square implies a product of two equal numbers while determination of the volume of a cube requires the product of three equal numbers. In reverse operation, determination of the side of a square given the area and that of a cube given the volume requires the determination of numbers we call square roots and cube roots respectively. To be able to work on such and similar problems, we require to know how to work with these number representations along with others (representations). We are also going to look at scientific forms, percentages and ratios. We will also look at situations where these are used, that is, in numerical expressions, real life problems involving proportions and ratios, commission, simple interest, markups, markdowns, tax and gratuities.

SQUARES AND SQUARE ROOTS

When a number is written in the form a^2 where a any number is, we say it is a square for a and we refer to a or $-a$ as its square root. a^2 implies $a \times a$. For example $16 = 4 \times 4 = 4^2$, hence the square of 4 is 16 while the square root of 16 is 4 or -4. In this section, we are going to write numerical expressions in terms of square roots and squares of numbers.

EXAMPLE 1 ....

Express the number $121 - 98 + 28$ in terms of squares of numbers.

EXPLANATION

$$121 = 11 \times 11 = 11^2$$
$$98 = 2 \times 49 = 2 \times 7^2$$
$$28 = 4 \times 7 = 2^2 \times 7$$

EXAMPLE 2

Express the number $72 - \sqrt{18} + 25$ in terms of squares and square roots of numbers.

EXPLANATION

$$72 = 2 \times 36$$

Since $36 = 6 \times 6 = 6^2$, we have $72 = 2 \times 6^2$

$18 = 2 \times 9$ hence

$$\sqrt{18} = \sqrt{2 \times 9} = \sqrt{2} \times \sqrt{9} = \sqrt{2} \times 3 = 3\sqrt{2}$$
$$25 = 5 \times 5 = 5^2$$

Hence $72 - \sqrt{18} + 25 = (2 \times 6^2) - 3\sqrt{2} + 5^2$

EXAMPLE 3..

Express the number $54(8 + \sqrt{20}) - 75$ in terms of squares and square roots of numbers.

EXPLANATION

$$54 = 6 \times 9 = 6 \times 3^2$$
$$8 = 2 \times 4 = 2 \times 2^2$$
$$\sqrt{20} = \sqrt{4 \times 5} = \sqrt{4} \times \sqrt{5} = 2\sqrt{5}$$
$$75 = 3 \times 25 = 3 \times 5^2$$
$$54\left(8 + \sqrt{20}\right) - 75 = \left(6 \times 3^2\right)\left(\left(2 \times 2^2\right) + 2\sqrt{5}\right) - (3 \times 5^2)$$

CUBES & CUBE ROOTS

A cube is a product of three numbers that are equal. The cube root of a number is a number such that when multiplied three times by itself, we get the former number. The cube of a number x is denoted by x^2 while the cube root of a number x is denoted by $\sqrt[3]{x}$. Example, the cube of 3 is $3^3 = 3 \times 3 \times 3 = 27$. The cube root of 27 is $\sqrt[3]{27} = 3$. In this section, we are going to write numerical expressions in terms of cubes and cube roots of numbers.

EXAMPLE 1 ....

Express $8 - 2(54 - 64)$ as sum, difference and product of cube of numbers.

EXPLANATION

$$8 = 2 \times 2 \times 2 = 2^3$$
$$54 = 2 \times 27 = 2 \times 3 \times 3 \times 3 = 2 \times 3^3$$
$$64 = 4 \times 4 \times 4 = 4^3$$

Thus, we have

$$8 - 2\left(54 - 64\right) = 2^3 - 2\left(\left(2 \times 3^3\right) - \left(4^3\right)\right)$$

EXAMPLE 2 ....

Express $\sqrt[3]{72} - 4\left(\dfrac{108}{343} + \sqrt[3]{128}\right)$ in terms of cube and cube roots of numbers.

EXPLANATION

$$\sqrt[3]{72} = \sqrt[3]{8 \times 9} = \sqrt[3]{8} \times \sqrt[3]{9} = 2\sqrt[3]{9}$$
$$108 = 4 \times 27 = 4 \times 3^3$$
$$343 = 7^3$$
$$128 = 2 \times 64 = 2 \times 4^3$$

Thus

$$\sqrt[3]{128} = \sqrt[3]{2 \times 4^3} = \sqrt[3]{2} \times \sqrt[3]{4^3} = 4\sqrt[3]{2}$$

Upon substitution, we have

$$\sqrt[3]{72} - 4\left(\frac{108}{343} + \sqrt[3]{128}\right) = 2\sqrt[3]{9} - 4\left(\frac{4 \times 3^3}{7^3} + 4\sqrt[3]{2}\right)$$

EXAMPLE 3...

Express $\dfrac{8}{\sqrt[3]{40}} - 48 - \sqrt[3]{192}$ in terms of cube and cube roots of numbers.

EXPLANATION

$$8 = 2^3$$
$$40 = 8 \times 5 = \sqrt[3]{8 \times 5} = \sqrt[3]{8} \times \sqrt[3]{5} = 2\sqrt[3]{5}$$
$$48 = 8 \times 6 = 2^3 \times 6$$
$$192 = 64 \times 3 = \sqrt[3]{64 \times 3} = \sqrt[3]{64} \times \sqrt[3]{3} = 4\sqrt[3]{3}$$
$$\frac{8}{\sqrt[3]{40}} - 48 - \sqrt[3]{192} = \frac{2^3}{2\sqrt[3]{5}} - \left(2^3 \times 6\right) - 4\sqrt[3]{3}$$

SCIENTIFIC NOTATIONS, ONE OR MULTI-STEP PROBLEMS

A number is written in scientific notation if it is in the form $A + 10^b$ where A is a decimal number between 1 and 10, n is an integer expect zero and b represents the number of steps through which a decimal is moved to have the number A. The number b is negative if the decimal is moved in positive direction, in the right hand side direction and positive if the decimal is moved in negative direction, in the left hand side direction.

For example, $0.00597313 = 5.973 \times 10^{-3}$ in standard form (written to 4 significant figures)

$8127745 = 8.128 \times 10^6$ in standard form (written to 4 significant figures)

In this section, we are going to simplify real world problems involving scientific notation.

EXAMPLE 1 ....

A company manufactures 4713900 beads every day. If they are packed in 30 packet each having an equal number of beads, how many beads does each packet have? Write you answer in scientific notation.

EXPLANATION

Total number of beads = 4713900

Number of packets = 30

Number of beads in each packet =

$$\frac{4713900}{30} = 157,130$$

We convert 157130 to scientific notation. The decimal in the number 157130, is after zero, to achieve a number between 1 and 10 from 157130, we move the decimal point the left between 1 and 5. The decimal would have moved 5 steps, hence $b = 5$ and $A = 1.57130 \cong 1.571$ to four significant figures.

Thus, number of beads in each packet is 1.571×10^5.

EXAMPLE 2 ....

A company has four departments where each uses 1080 quarts, 2018 quarts, 1876 quarts and 2000 quarts respectively per day. If the company pays $0.94 per 1000 quarts, find amount of money the company pays every month given that it operates on an average of 26 days a month. Write you answer in scientific form.

EXPLANATION

The total capacity of water used in a day is $1080 + 2018 + 1876 + 2000 = 6974$ quarts

The capacity used per month is $6974 \times 26 = 181324$ quarts

1000 quarts is equivalent to $0.94

181324 quarts will be equivalent to

$$181324 \times \frac{0.94}{1000} \cong \$170.4$$

$$170.4 = \$1.704 \times 10^2$$

UNITS OF MEASURE

Ratios refers to a comparison of quantities that have the same characteristics. For instance, one may compare the age of two different people. The ratio of one item h to another is given by h to k, $h : k$ or $\frac{h}{k}$.

Proportion refers to an equation where two ratios are equated. We may have direct or indirect or inverse proportion. In this section, we are going to deal with problems on ratio and proportion which in involves conversion of one unit to another.

EXAMPLE 1 ....

The ratio of the weights of two students is 11: 10. If the weight of the lighter student is 80 pounds, find the weight of the heavier one in stones.

EXPLANATION

The ratio of two students = 11.10

The fraction of the lighter one is $\frac{10}{21}$

This is equivalent to 80 pounds

The total weight of the students

$$\frac{21}{10} \times 80 = 168 \text{ pounds}$$

We convert to stones

$$1 \text{ stone} = 14 \text{ pounds}$$
$$168 \text{ pounds} = \frac{168}{14} = 12 \text{ stones}$$

EXAMPLE 2..

The price of two gallons of gasoline is $4.34. Johnston's car has 12 quarts of gasoline. If his journey requires 34 quarts of gasoline, how much more is he required to spend to be able to go for the journey?

EXPLANATION

Capacity of gasoline to be added = 34 − 12 = 22 quarts

$$4 \text{ quarts} = 1 \text{ gallon}$$

$$22 \text{ quarts} = \frac{22 \times 1}{4} = 5.5 \text{ gallons}$$

We determine the amount to be spent

2 gallons are equivalent to $4.34

5.5 gallons will be equivalent to

$$\frac{4.34 \times 5.5}{2} = \$11.935$$

SIMPLE INTEREST, TAX, MARKUPS & MARKDOWNS, GRATUITIES, COMMISSIONS, % INCREASE AND % DECREASE

When finds are deposited in any financial institution, it earns extra money computed as a percentage of that deposited. This extra money is called an interest. For simple interest, S.I, we have $S.I = p \times \frac{r}{100} \times t$ where p called principle is the amount deposited, r and t are the rate and the period for which the deposited amount grows.

Tax is the amount a government levies on a given good or service rendered.

Markup and markdowns refers to an increase and a decrease in price respectively.

Gratuity is a gratitude that a worker gets after performing a certain job while commission is money that a person earns after making a sale.

In this section, we look at examples having such problems whose change is expressed in terms of a percentage.

EXAMPLE 1 ....

The price of a bicycle was $200. If there was a 15% mark up, determine the new price.

EXPLANATION

The original price $200

The markup = 15%

The markup in dollars is

$$\frac{15}{100} \times 200 = \$30$$

The new price = $200 + 30 = $230.

EXAMPLE 2 ....

A salesperson earns a commission of 24% on goods sold worthy $350 and an extra 15% on each of $20 sold above $350. In a given day, the salesperson made a sale worth $490. Determine the commission earned.

EXPLANATION

First commission earned is

$$\frac{24}{100} \times 350 = \$84$$

The amount remaining after $350 is 490 − 350 = $410

The extra commission earned is

$$\frac{15}{100} \times 140 = \$21$$

The total commission is given by $21 + $84 = $105

EXAMPLE 3..

A farm owner increases the length of the rectangular piece of land allocated for dairy farming by 20%. If the new length is 24yards and the width is 10 yards, determine the original dimensions.

EXPLANATION

Increase in length is 20% of / were / is the original length.

The new length is equivalent to 100 + 20% = 120%

The original length is 100%

$$\text{Original length} = \frac{100}{120} \times 24 = 20$$

Original dimension is 20 yards by 10 yards

EXAMPLE 4..

A company makes a profit of $720000 before tax in a year. If the tax is 44%. Determine their actual profit, after tax.

EXPLANATION

$$\text{Tax} = \frac{44}{100} \times 720000 = \$316800$$

Profit after tax = 720000 − 316800 = $403200

WRAPPING IT UP

In this section, we have looked at different forms of representing numerical numbers that is using squares, cubes, square roots and cube roots. We have also looked at a scientific notation which is the standard way of representing numerical numbers in scientific papers. Apart from representation of numbers, we have considered problem involving a change of units of measurements from one form to another. Finally, we have looked at problems involving percentage representation such as markups, markdowns, commissions, gratuity, tax, simple interest and percentage change.

GLOSSARY

- ❏ **Ascending orders:** Implies arranging numbers from the lowest to the highest.

- ❏ **Bar graph:** Is a graph that is composed of bars whose heights are proportional to the frequency of items in data.

- ❏ **Box plot:** Is a graphical representations inform of a box where the end of the box represents the lower and upper quarter while a line inside the box represents the median of the data.

- ❏ **Central angle:** Is an angle formed by two intersecting radii such that its vertex is at the center of the circle.

- ❏ **Circle graph:** Is a circular representation of data where data items take proportional shapes of the circle.

- ❏ **Circumference of a circle:** The distance covered around a circle.

- ❏ **Combination:** Is an arrangement of items where order is not necessary.

- ❏ **Composite geometric figures:** A plane figures that are composed of more than one basic geometric figure.

- ❏ **Cone:** It is a prism having a circular base and a curved surface

- ❏ **Coordinates of a point on XY plane:** It is the distance of a point from an axis on xy plane.

- ❏ **Cube root of a number:** Is a number such that when multiplied three times by itself, we get the former.

- ❏ **Cube:** Is a product of three numbers that are equal.

- ❏ **Cylinder:** A three dimensional figure with a curved surface that is enclosed by two circular faces at the top and the bottom.

- ❏ **Descending order:** Implies writing numbers from the highest.

- ❏ **Diameter:** A straight line from one side of the circle to the other that passes through the center.

❏ **Direct proportion:** It is a situation where an increase (decrease) in one variable leads to an increase (decrease) of the other.

❏ **Domain:** Is the collection of all inputs of a function.

❏ **Dot plots:** Is a kind of graphical representation where frequency is represented by the number of dots.

❏ **Equation of a line:** It is a relation showing the collection of all points lying on the line.

❏ **Equilateral triangle:** It is a triangle where all sides are equal.

❏ **Exponential form:** A number is written in an exponential notation if it is in the form a^b where a is the base and b the exponent.

❏ **Factors**: Are numbers that divides other numbers.

❏ **Gratuity:** Is a gratitude that a worker gets after performing a certain job while commission is money that a person earns after making a sale.

❏ **Histogram:** Is a graph that is composed on bars that are in contact with each other and whose height is proportional to the frequency of the items represented.

❏ **Intercept:** It is a point where the line intersects the axis of a plane (such as xy plane).

❏ **Inverse proportion:** It is a situation where an increase (decrease) in one variable leads to a decrease (increase) of the other.

❏ **Isosceles Triangle:** It is a triangle where two sides are equal.

❏ **Linear equations:** Refers to a composition of an expression in one unknown that is equated to a number.

❏ **Linear expressions with rational coefficients:** Are symbolic representations of quantifiable mathematical statements whose coefficients are fractions.

❏ **Linear expressions**: Are algebraic expressions where the highest power of the independent variable, the x variable, is 1.

❏ **Linear function:** Is an equation where a variable, the dependent variable (say y), is expressed in terms in terms of another, independent variable (say x), with the former having the highest power of 1.

❏ **Linear functions:** Are relations whose graphs are straight lines.

- ❏ **Markup and markdowns:** Refers to an increase and a decrease in price respectively.

- ❏ **Mean**: Refers to the sum of values divided by the number of these values.

- ❏ **Measures of central tendency:** Refers to the values of a given data that try to locate the center of the data, hence they are used as single representatives of a given data.

- ❏ **Median:** Is the middle value of the data when arranged in either ascending or descending order.

- ❏ **Mode:** Is the most common value in data.

- ❏ **Multiples**: Are numbers that are as a result of the product of a number with integers.

- ❏ **Multi-variable linear equations:** Are equations that have two or more variables (unknown) where the highest power on the variable is one.

- ❏ **Number:** Is written in scientific notation if it is in the form $A + 10^b$ where A is a decimal number between 1 and 10, n is an integer expect zero and b represents the number of steps through which a decimal is moved to have the number A.

- ❏ **Permutation**: Refers to the arrangement of items where order is required.

- ❏ **Polygon:** A geometric figure with three sides or more sides.

- ❏ **Polynomial:** It is an expression having one or more algebraic terms with positive integer powers on the variables.

- ❏ **Polynomials**: Are expressions with variables having integer powers.

- ❏ **Prime factors**: Are factors that are prime numbers.

- ❏ **Prime numbers**: Are numbers that can be divided by one and themselves.

- ❏ **Probability:** Is a measure of how certain an event is likely to occur.

- ❏ **Proportion:** A mathematical set up where two ratios are equated. Proportion also refers to a comparison of two items whose value increases as the other decreases or increases.

- ❏ **Pyramid**: It is a three dimensional figure having a base with vertical faces that have one common apex.

- **Pythagorean Theorem:** It is a relation relating length of the three sides of a right angle.

- **Quadratic equation:** Is an equation whose highest powers, degree, is 2. It is generally given in the form $ax^2 + bx + c = 0$ where a cannot be zero, a, b and c are real numbers.

- **Quadratic formula:** Based on the general quadratic equation $ax^2 + bx + c = 0$, above is given by:

$$x = \frac{-b \pm \sqrt{b^2 - 4ac}}{2a}$$

- **Quadratic function:** Is an equation where the highest power of the independent variable being 2. We may generally represent it as $f(x) = ax^2 + bx + c$. These functions express relations whose graphs are in the form of a curve.

- **Quartile:** Is a value that divides data into four equal parts.

- **Radius:** A straight line from the center of the circle to the arc of the circle.

- **Range:** Is the difference between the largest and smallest value of data.

- **Rate:** Refers to a comparison between two items that have different features. When the second item is a unit, the rate is called unit rate.

- **Ratio:** A quotient that of two items that are similar.

- **Rational coefficients and coefficients:** That is informed of a fraction.

- **Rational expressions:** Are expressions in form of a fraction where the numerator and the denominator is a polynomial.

- **Rational fractions:** Are expressions in form of a fraction where the numerator and the denominator are polynomials.

- **Rational numbers:** Are numbers written in the form $\frac{a}{b}$ where a and b are real numbers and b is not zero.

- **Ratios:** Refers to a comparison of quantities that have the same characteristics.

- **Rectangle:** It is a four sided polygon where opposite sides are parallel and equal and its sides intersect and right angles.

- ❏ **Rectangular prism:** A three dimensional figure with six faces that are all rectangles.

- ❏ **Right angle:** It is a triangle whose two lines intersect perpendicularly.

- ❏ **Scale factor**: Is a ratio comparing two measurements.

- ❏ **Scale**: Is a ratio comparing two lengths where (in most cases), the first length is given as one unit.

- ❏ **Scalene triangle:** It is a triangle where none of the sides are equal.

- ❏ **Scatter plot:** Is a linear graphical relationship of bivariate data.

- ❏ **Scientific Notation:** A number is written in scientific notation if it is in the form $A + 10^b$ where A is a decimal number between 1 and 10, n is an integer expect zero and b represents the number of steps through which a decimal is moved to have the number A.

- ❏ **Sector:** A figure that is enclosed by a two radii and an arc of the circle.

- ❏ **Simple interest:** In an amount earned on some funds deposited in a financial account. It is given by $S.I = p \times \frac{r}{100} \times t$ where p called principle is the about deposited, r and t are the rate and the period for which the deposited amount grows.

- ❏ **Slope:** It is the ratio of rise of rum of a line.

- ❏ **Sphere:** It a three dimensional figure inform of a ball.

- ❏ **Square root of a number**: Is a number whose product by itself is the former number.

- ❏ **Square**: Is a product of a number by itself.

- ❏ **Symmetry:** A curve is symmetric about a line if the half of the curve on one side of the line is equal and overlaps the other half on the other side of the line.

- ❏ **System of simultaneous linear equations**: Refers to a pair or more collections of linear equations that may have a common solution.

- ❏ **Tax**: Is the amount a government levies on a given good or service rendered.

- ❏ **Triangle:** It is a three sided polygon.